THE GOSPEL OF
JOHN

Finding Identity and Purpose

PARTICIPANT'S GUIDE

MATT WILLIAMS
General Editor

 HENDRICKSON PUBLISHERS ROSE PUBLISHING

The Gospel of John Participant's Guide
© 2019 Matt Williams
Rose Publishing, LLC
P. O. Box 3473
Peabody, Massachusetts 01961-3473 USA
www.hendricksonrose.com

Printed in the United States of America
010519VP

CONTENTS

ABOUT THIS STUDY

I have been teaching the gospel of John for over twenty years to thousands of students in both Spain and the USA. It is a dream fulfilled that I can now present the fruit of my studies to the local church in the form of this video series. May you encounter the same Jesus that we find in the gospel of John—the One who healed the sick, walked on water, preached the good news of the kingdom, and rose from the dead to provide a way to God the Father. My prayer is that you will respond the way my students have—with awe at the wonder of the Word of God, and with hearts and lives transformed by Jesus's life and ministry.

Who am I? What is my purpose? In *The Gospel of John: Finding Identity and Purpose* video Bible study, biblical scholars explain the deeper, first-century meaning of twelve passages from the gospel of John. Then, they give modern applications of the text in order to help us find our identity in Christ and our purpose in life. Through this study, you will learn that you are loved, restored, forgiven, a temple of the Holy Spirit, a light, and more.

So we invite you to come with us on an adventure! Let's look back to the first century in order to understand the biblical text—and then accurately apply it to our lives today in the twenty-first century. As we do so, may we find our identity and purpose.

A special thanks is due to Dr. Todd Bolen for the use of his Israel photos both in this participant's guide and in the video. As you will see, these photos help us to grasp the meaning of the text as we see sights from Israel where Jesus walked, taught, and ministered. I highly recommend his excellent resources at www.bibleplaces.com.

MATT WILLIAMS,
General Editor

MEET THE TEACHERS

DR. LEON HARRIS is an Assistant Professor of Theology at Talbot School of Theology, Biola University. He graduated from the University of Aberdeen in Scotland with a PhD in Divinity. His most recent publication is *The Holy Spirit as Communion*. Dr. Harris has also presented several papers at theology conferences both in the U.K. and the U.S. His current research interests include Pneumatology, Black theology, and Relational Ontology.

DR. JOANNE JUNG is Associate Dean and Associate Professor of Biblical and Theological Studies at Talbot School of Theology. She authored *Knowing Grace: Cultivating a Lifestyle of Godliness*; *Godly Conversation: Rediscovering the Puritan Practice of Conference*; *Character Formation in Online Education*; and *The Lost Discipline of Conversation: Surprising Lessons in Spiritual Formation Drawn from the English Puritans*.

DR. SEAN MCDOWELL is a professor of Christian Apologetics at Biola University, the National Spokesman for Summit Ministries, a popular speaker, part-time high school teacher, and best-selling author or co-author of over 18 books including *Evidence That Demands A Verdict*. Follow him on Twitter: @sean_mcdowell and his blog: seanmcdowell.org.

DR. MARK STRAUSS is University Professor of New Testament at Bethel Seminary in San Diego. He is the author of many books and articles, including commentaries on the gospels of Mark and Luke and *Four Portraits, One Jesus: A Survey of Jesus and the Gospels*. In addition, he serves as Vice Chair of the Committee on Bible Translation for the *New International Version* and is a frequent preacher and teacher in San Diego area churches.

DR. JEREMY TREAT (PhD, Wheaton College) is pastor for preaching and vision at Reality LA and adjunct professor of theology at Biola University. He is the author of *The Crucified King: Atonement and Kingdom in Biblical and Systematic Theology*.

DR. MATT WILLIAMS is professor and department chair of New Testament at Talbot School of Theology. He is author and editor of six other video Bible studies: Parables, Miracles, Prayers, Life, Last Days, and Forgiveness of Jesus; along with *What the New Testament Authors Really Cared About*, and two books on the Gospels. As a former missionary to Spain, he has edited 62 books in Spanish: *Comentarios Bíblicos con Aplicación: Nueva Versión Internacional, Biblioteca Teológica Vida*, and *Colección Teológica Contemporánea*.

HOST: BRUCE MARCHIANO is an actor best known for his film portrayal of Jesus in *The Visual Bible: The Gospel of Matthew* and many other Christian films, including *The Encounter, Allison's Choice*, and the upcoming Gospel of John video. Bruce is the author of several books on the person of Jesus, including the best-selling *In the Footsteps of Jesus*, and the founder of Marchiano Ministries, an outreach ministry serving primarily in southern Africa.

CALLED TO HONOR
Water to Wine

◇

DR. SEAN MCDOWELL

JOHN 2:1–11

*What Jesus did here in Cana of Galilee was the first
of the signs through which he revealed his glory;
and his disciples believed in him.*

John 2:11

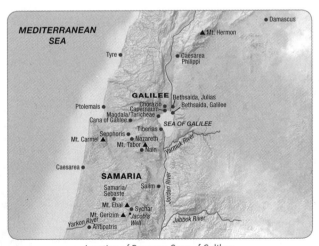

Location of Passage: Cana of Galilee;
Kefar Kenna (traditional site), Khirbet Qana (probable site)

PART 1: DIGGING FOR MEANING

While many Christians read this passage simply as an amazing miracle of changing water to wine, once we understand the Old Testament background and Jewish messianic expectations, we see that this incredible miracle shows us exactly who Jesus is and why he came.

Video Introduction by Bruce Marchiano
Video Scripture Reading: John 2:1-11

◆ Identity issues

◆ Jesus performs his first miracle by changing water into wine.

Turned water into wine so good that it horrored them.

The Old Testament background shows us two key points:

◇ Jesus is the Messiah who is bringing the new covenant.

◇ Jesus is saving this wedding family from severe shame.

Amos

◆ Ceremonial washing

Stone water jars, first century AD

> The Pharisees and all the Jews do not eat unless they give their hands a ceremonial washing, holding to the tradition of the elders.
>
> Mark 7:3

◆ Significance of wine in the Old Testament

> On this mountain the LORD Almighty will prepare a feast of rich food for all peoples, a banquet of aged wine—the best of meats and the finest of wines.
>
> Isaiah 25:6

◆ Wine as a symbol of the coming new covenant: Davidic kingdom

> *In that day I will restore David's fallen shelter—I will repair its broken walls and restore its ruins—and will rebuild it as it used to be.*
>
> Amos 9:11

◆ God will send a messianic King in the line of David.

> *"The days are coming," declares the LORD, "when the reaper will be overtaken by the plowman and the planter by the one treading grapes. New wine will drip from the mountains and flow from all the hills."*
>
> Amos 9:13

◆ Significance of weddings

> *As a young man marries a young woman, so will your Builder [God] marry you; as a bridegroom rejoices over his bride, so will your God rejoice over you.*
>
> Isaiah 62:5

◆ Meaning of Jesus turning water to wine:

Jesus is the Messiah, the Son of David, who comes to fulfill and restore Judaism and bring the expected kingdom of God.

◆ Deeper meaning: running out of wine in an honor/shame culture

"To run out of wine was not simply a social embarrassment but entailed a serious loss of family honour."

—Andrew Lincoln[2]

◆ Jesus saves the wedding family from their *shame*.

> *Then he called the bridegroom aside and said, "Everyone brings out the choice wine first and then the cheaper wine after the guests have had too much to drink; but you have saved the best till now."*
>
> John 2:9–10

◆ Jesus gives *honor* to this wedding family.

> *The LORD your God is with you, the Mighty Warrior who saves. He will take great delight in you; in his love he will no longer rebuke you but will rejoice over you with singing. I will remove from you all who mourn over the loss of your appointed festivals, which is a burden and reproach for you. At that time I will deal with all who oppressed you. I will rescue the lame; I will gather the exiles. I will give them praise and honor in every land where they have suffered shame.*
>
> Zephaniah 3:17–19

14

Discussion #1

1. What is the Old Testament expectation for wine? Imagine that you were a Jewish waiter working at the wedding in Cana, and saw Jesus turn the water into wine. Do you think that you would have understood the significance of the miracle?

2. John 2:11 says, "What Jesus did here in Cana of Galilee was the first of the signs through which he revealed his glory; and his disciples believed in him." How do you think that most people in the church today define *belief* in Jesus?

3. Jesus removes shame and brings honor to the wedding family by providing the "best" wine. What types of shame do you think people in the church carry today? What would it be like if Jesus miraculously removed all shame from the church and turned that shame into honor, as Zephaniah prophesies?

PART 2: YOUR LIFE TODAY

This is a powerful miracle about God rescuing a family from shame through turning water into wine, but also about Jesus revealing his identity as the Messiah who restores Judaism and brings the expected kingdom of God.

What does it mean to believe in Jesus?

> "When Jesus speaks for the last time, he says, 'Follow me.' . . . To relate to Jesus is to go with him. The call to faith is a call to a way of life."
>
> —Craig Koester[3]

◇ Faith in Jesus leads to faithfulness.

> Jesus replied: "Love the Lord your God with all your heart and with all your soul and with all your mind."
>
> Matthew 22:37

◆ From shame to honor

◇ Our experience of guilt and shame

Sean McDowell and his father
Josh McDowell

"Son, I refuse to see myself as 'used goods.' God loves me, forgives me, and can use me to bless others."

—Josh McDowell

◇ Jesus cares for us enough to take our shame away.

See, I lay a stone in Zion, a chosen and precious cornerstone, and the one who trusts in him will never be put to shame.

1 Peter 2:6

◇ God gives us honor.

What is our *identity* as Christians?

◇ We are believers in Jesus.

◇ We are honored by God.

What is our *purpose* as his followers?

◇ Those who are honored show honor to others.

> "The 'world' . . . is in darkness, is ruled by a demonic power, is alienated from God and his agents, and is morally opposed to Jesus. . . . Still, it is the object of God's saving love and enlightenment in Jesus."
>
> —Craig Keener[4]

Who do you know in your sphere of influence that is struggling?

What are you waiting for?

Discussion #2

1. In Discussion #1, we talked about types of shame that people carry today. How have you seen people deal with their shame? Is it more common to hide it, confess it, do good works to outweigh it, or to ask Jesus to carry it for them?

   Substance abuse – Don't share much about themselves.

2. What would it look like if we today offered our shame to Jesus, for him to carry? What has worked for you in your past experiences?

   It would free so many people up spiritually

3. Do you feel that God *honors* you? Why or why not? How can we let the truth of this honor sink into our lives more?

   God honors us by taking our sins.

4. Sean McDowell asked, "Who do you know in your sphere of influence that is struggling?" Take a few moments to think of both nonbelievers and Christians who are struggling with shame. How could you help them this week to go to Jesus for relief from that burden?

5. Take some time to pray as you end the study.

PERSONAL REFLECTION

Day One

1. Read John 2:1–11.

2. Let's focus today on shame. Do you believe that Jesus wants to take away shame from you? Why or why not?

3. Reflect about the areas that you feel guilt and shame, and talk to God about it (usually these are the things we try not to think about). Are there repercussions from your past that you are still carrying with you? What is weighing you down?

4. Pray about the shame that you feel. How is carrying your shame still impacting/damaging you? Do you think that Jesus wants you to continue to carry that shame, or is it time to leave it at the cross for Jesus to carry? (See Matthew 11:28.)

5. Begin to memorize the key verse for this passage: John 2:11.

Day Two

1. Read Zephaniah 3:19–20.

2. Let's focus today on honor. God not only removes our shame but gives us great honor. In what ways has God shown you honor in the past?

3. How is God showing you honor in the present? Think about family, friends, job, ministry, etc.

4. How will God show you honor in the future (think about eternity)?

5. Take some time to thank God for what he has done, will do, and is doing in your life.

Day Three

1. Read 1 Peter 2:6.

2. Let's focus today on Sean McDowell's last words in the video, "God desires that we become his agents who bring honor to a hurting and broken world. What are you waiting for?" What do you think this means?

3. Who in your life needs to experience Jesus's honor instead of shame? How can you help them this week to take steps toward this freedom from shame? Can you think of specific words you could say to them or actions you could take? Think both of simple, easy things you can do, and also harder things you could do.

4. As you think about ministry, consider both those who are *physically* poor and those who are *spiritually* poor. Are there people in your life who have all of life's pleasures, but are spiritually poor? What could you do to reach these people in your sphere of influence?

Day Four

1. Read Isaiah 66:19.

2. Let's focus today on our calling to the whole world. An interesting fact is that most of the Old Testament prophecies that talk about the coming wine in the new covenant also talk about "all nations" or "all peoples." (Read Isaiah 25:6; Jeremiah 31:10, 31; and Amos 9:12 to see this.) Why is this significant?

3. What might the Jewish people in Jesus's time have thought about the nations (also called the gentiles)? Would it have been positive or negative?

4. The world needs to hear about the forgiveness of Jesus and his removal of shame from their lives. How might you show interest in helping others and the world (nations)?

Day Five

1. Read John 2:1–11 one more time.

2. Pray through the entire passage verse by verse, allowing the deeper meaning that you have discovered lead you as you pray. Ask the Spirit to continue to remind you of what you have learned and to help you apply these truths to your life. Jot down any further applications that come to mind as you pray.

3. Turn back to the discussion questions from the video teaching (Discussion #1, #2). If there are questions that your group didn't have time to discuss or questions that you might like to think more about, use this time to review and reflect further.

CALLED TO BELONG
Temple Cleansing

◇

DR. LEON HARRIS

JOHN 2:13–22

*To those who sold doves he said, "Get these out of here!
Stop turning my Father's house into a market!"*

John 2:16

Location of Passage: Jerusalem Temple

PART 1: DIGGING FOR MEANING

Jesus is correcting the injustice of insiders versus outsiders.

Video Introduction by Bruce Marchiano
Video Scripture Reading: John 2:13–22

◆ Outsiders in Scotland

Banoffee pie

◆ Background of the Jewish temple

◆ Solomon included foreigners in his prayer.

> As for the foreigner who does not belong to your people
> Israel but has come from a distant land because of your
> name . . . Do whatever the foreigner asks of you, so that
> all the peoples of the earth may know your name and fear
> you, as do your own people Israel, and may know that this
> house I have built bears your Name.
>
> 1 Kings 8:41–43

◆ Israel did not honor this prayer.

◆ Unity and diversity: outsiders

◆ Jesus arrives at the temple.

Did You Know?

Passover was one of the three annual feasts that required the presence in Jerusalem of every Jewish male twelve years of age and older (see Deut. 16:16).[5]

◆ Court of the Gentiles

In this temple model, the Court of the Gentiles is shown as the large flat area inside the walls of the temple complex.

◆ Jesus's zeal: God's house as a place for all people

> "For any Gentile who came up to the temple to worship it meant that prayer had to be offered in the middle of a cattle yard and money market."
>
> —Leon Morris[6]

◆ Injustice: denying access to gentiles

> And foreigners who bind themselves to the LORD. . . . Their burnt offerings and sacrifices will be accepted on my altar; for my house will be called a house of prayer for all nations.
>
> Isaiah 56:6–7

◆ Jesus was cleaning house.

> Zeal for your house consumes me.
>
> Psalm 69:9

◆ Jesus cares about sin.

> *Will you steal and murder, commit adultery and perjury, burn incense to Baal and follow other gods you have not known, and then come and stand before me in this house, which bears my Name, and say, "We are safe"—safe to do all these detestable things? Has this house, which bears my Name, become a den of robbers to you? But I have been watching! declares the LORD.*
>
> Jeremiah 7:9–11

◆ Judgment for Israel's hypocrisy

> *A day of the LORD is coming. . . . And on that day there will no longer be a Canaanite [trader] in the house of the LORD Almighty.*
>
> Zechariah 14:1, 21b

◆ Fighting for control to discriminate

◆ A parable

> *Jesus answered them, "Destroy this temple, and I will raise it again in three days." They replied, "It has taken forty-six years to build this temple, and you are going to raise it in three days?" But the temple he had spoken of was his body.*
>
> John 2:19–21

◆ The meaning of the parable

> *"The temple was where sacrifices were offered for sin. Jesus is the ultimate sacrifice, the sacrifice offered once and for all for the sins of the whole world."*
>
> —Matt Carter and Josh Wredberg[7]

Discussion #1

1. Based on what you know about the Old Testament, why do you think the Jewish people of Jesus's day would exclude the gentiles? Who are the "outsiders" for today's church? Maybe the church does not do it on purpose, but do you think there are things that we do that unintentionally exclude outsiders?

2. What do you think Solomon is asking God to do in his prayer in 1 Kings 8:41–43? Is he asking for miracles? Should we pray this way in our prayers?

3. Both Zechariah 14 and Jeremiah 7 talk about judgment for those who are not following the Lord. Jesus cleaned out the temple as a symbol of this judgment. If Jesus came to your church, what sorts of practices and attitudes would he need to clean out? What if he came to investigate *your* heart; what kinds of things would he need to clean out?

PART 2: YOUR LIFE TODAY

By turning over the tables, Jesus overturns the tables of separation and announces, "Welcome home" to outsiders.

◆ Insiders vs. outsiders

◆ Jesus alone defines who is "in."

Warning posted at entrance to temple: "No foreigner is to go beyond the balustrade and the plaza of the temple zone. Whoever is caught doing so will have himself to blame for his death which will follow."

Yet to all who received him, to those who believed in his name, he gave the right to become children of God.

John 1:12

◆ Welcome Home!

For I am not ashamed of the gospel, because it is the power of God that brings salvation to everyone who believes: first to the Jew, then to the Gentile. For in the gospel the righteousness of God is revealed—a righteousness that is by faith from first to last, just as it is written: "The righteous will live by faith."

Romans 1:16–17

◆ Passive side: We belong!

> *"When Jesus halted 'trade' in the temple, he alluded to a portion of Scripture that envisioned all nations worshiping in Jerusalem (Zech 14:16)."*
>
> —Craig Koester[8]

◆ Active side: Our responsibility

◆ A kingdom that is united

◆ Love one another in unity.

> *"If Jesus were to arrive at a church in my city, would he build a whip out of pew rope or would he praise God for what is happening there?"*
>
> —Gary Burge[9]

◆ God loves you: you are an insider.

◆ Reconciliation with God

◆ Reconciliation between diverse groups

Discussion #2

1. What would our churches be like today if every church had the motto, _Welcome Home?_ How would this affect your church and your city?

2. Have you ever been (or are now) part of a multiethnic church? If so, what was/is it like? What can you and your church do to increase reconciliation between diverse groups?

3. Jesus is bringing justice to those who were trying to exclude the gentiles. In what way can our churches today help bring justice in our communities?

4. Since this passage shows us that we belong and that God desires to welcome us home, take some time in prayer individually and then as a group to once again draw near to God's throne of grace through the blood of Jesus. Confess any sins that come to mind and rejoice in a God who loves us so much that he carries our sins for us. Enjoy his "hug" today. You belong!

PERSONAL REFLECTION

Day One

1. Read John 2:13–22.

2. Is there something in your past that causes you to feel that God will not accept you? To make you feel as though you are a foreigner, an outsider? Take some time and allow the Spirit to bring to mind any barriers that are keeping you from feeling close to your Savior.

3. Are there areas of your life which you have presumed or continue to presume upon God's grace?

4. If you saw yourself as God sees you, do you think that you would continue to struggle with the same sins? Why or why not?

5. Begin to memorize the key verse for this passage: John 2:16.

Day Two

1. Read Matthew 21:12–17.

2. It's clear in both the water-to-wine passage and here in the temple cleansing that God is interested in welcoming home the entire world! Are there ways that you hinder others from coming to know God?

3. Do we have an interest in the nations as Jesus shows us here in John? Jesus put his own life in danger by protecting the rights of these gentiles to worship. Are we willing to do this? Can you think of sacrifices that you could make in order to reach others with the gospel?

4. Jesus cleansed the temple because he had zeal for God's holiness, but also to protect others' rights. He was acting in the name of justice and righteousness, as he was fighting injustice toward the gentiles, those who were seen as outcasts/outsiders. Who are the "outcasts" today, and what could we do to fight against the injustices that they experience?

Day Three

1. Read Mark 11:15–18.

2. Read Jeremiah 7:1–20 (Jesus quotes verse 11). What was the issue that caused Jeremiah, and Jesus, to act? Do you see this same type of hypocrisy in the church today—people coming to church who have no intention of really repenting of their sin?

3. We sometimes forget that God is holy. Just as the Israelites needed to offer sacrifices to God at the temple, what sacrifices do we offer to him today? (See Romans 12:1.)

Day Four

1. Read Luke 19:45–47.

2. The high ethics of the Jewish people attracted many gentiles to the temple to worship the God of Israel. Are non-christians attracted to our churches because of what they see? What can we do to improve our reputation in the world in order to attract others to Jesus, as John 17:23 says?

3. The glory of God is no longer found in the Jerusalem temple, but in the fulfillment of this temple, in a person—in Jesus, and ultimately in the "temples" of God, us believers (1 Corinthians 6:19). How are you doing at reflecting his glory in your life? Spend some time meditating about this idea.

Day Five

1. Read John 2:13–22 one more time.

2. Pray through the entire passage verse by verse, allowing the deeper meaning that you have discovered lead you as you pray. Ask the Spirit to continue to remind you of what you have learned and to help you apply these truths to your life. Jot down any further applications that come to mind as you pray.

3. Turn back to the discussion questions from the video teaching (Discussion #1, #2). If there are questions that your group did not have time to discuss or questions that you might like to think more about, use this time to review and reflect further.

CALLED TO BELIEVE
Nicodemus

◇

DR. JOANNE JUNG

JOHN 3:1–16

*For God so loved the world that he gave his one
and only Son, that whoever believes in him shall
not perish but have eternal life.*

John 3:16

Location of Passage: Jerusalem at night

PART 1: DIGGING FOR MEANING

God demonstrates his love for all of us by giving his Son. The Messiah is God's gift to the world.

Video Introduction by Bruce Marchiano
Video Scripture Reading: John 3:1–16

◈ John 3:16

◈ Pharisees

> "Nicodemus stands as the representative of the old religion."
> —Leon Morris[10]

◈ Keeping the Sabbath day holy

cut hair
pull hair from head
no more than 1 letter
can't cut fingernails

◆ Nicodemus, a Pharisee

John 3:1
a Jewish Leader
Commanded respect
He was rich, powerful,
He respects Jesus.
He seeks answers
Water for pure at Heart.
Spirit for transformation

Did You Know?

Nicodemus was part of the Gurion family, one of the wealthiest and most powerful of lay aristocratic families represented on the governing high priest's council.[11]

◆ Jesus explains the Christian system.

He came to Jesus at night and said, "Rabbi, we know that you are a teacher who has come from God. For no one could perform the signs you are doing if God were not with him."

John 3:2

◆ Nicodemus is seeking answers.

> **Did You Know?**
>
> The Greek term *anwthen* can mean "born again" or "born from above."[12]

Jesus replied, "Very truly I tell you, no one can see the kingdom of God unless they are born again." "How can someone be born when they are old?" Nicodemus asked. "Surely they cannot enter a second time into their mother's womb to be born!"

John 3:3–4

◆ Nicodemus doesn't understand Ezekiel 36.

"They believed that Israelites did not need this transformation. . . . It is therefore not surprising that Nicodemus might not grasp what Jesus was demanding of him."

—Craig Keener[13]

I will sprinkle clean water on you, and you will be clean; I will cleanse you from all your impurities and from all your idols. I will give you a new heart and put a new spirit in you; I will remove from you your heart of stone and give you a heart of flesh. And I will put my Spirit in you and move you to follow my decrees and be careful to keep my laws.

Ezekiel 36:25–27

◆ Faith/belief in Jesus

Just as Moses lifted up the snake in the wilderness, so the Son of Man must be lifted up, that everyone who believes may have eternal life in him.

John 3:14–15

◆ John 3:16

For God so loved the world that he gave his one and only Son, that whoever believes in him shall not perish but have eternal life.

John 3:16

◆ Eternal life: quantity and quality

> *"The important thing about eternal life is not its quantity but its quality."*
>
> —Leon Morris[14]

◆ Whoever . . .

◆ Faith in Jesus is the determining factor.

Discussion #1

1. Based on John 3:16, what is the motivating factor that moves
    God to send Jesus? Is the definition of love in John 3:16 the same
    definition of love that we find in the world today? How is it
    different and/or similar? *Some places*

    *Humanity
    Love of the world*

2. What do you think are the main similarities and differences
    between Nicodemus's view of salvation or faith, and the Christian
    view, such as in John 3:16?

    *He had to earn it.
    If you did such + such, then you're in.
    Awe + Respect for God*

3. God is actively seeking the "whoevers" in the world. Who are the
    "whoevers" in your life that God might be seeking?

4. John 3 clearly shows us that God loves the world. Sometimes
    people conclude that since God loves the world, all will be saved
    and enter heaven. Based on John 3, does God's love for the world
    mean that everyone will be saved? Based on this Bible passage, what
    determines whether or not one will enter the kingdom of God?

    *You have to professit.
    Available to all but you have to take it.*

PART 2: YOUR LIFE TODAY

How will you ready yourself to share the gift you have freely received, and now is to be freely given?

◆ God is actively seeking. to who evers
in the world -
Grace, mercy, complete
+ Kindness

◆ Phone call
God loves you
God loves you, do you know that?

◆ Good news is for all.
is to share with everyone
Share freely with those around.

> ### Did You Know?
> Judaism rarely (or never) spoke of God's loving the world outside of Israel.[15]

◆ Sharing the message . . .

> "Nowhere in [John's] Gospel does God say, 'I love you'; rather, he demonstrates his love for humanity by self-sacrifice . . . and demands the same practical demonstration of love from his followers."
>
> —Craig Keener[16]

◆ . . . with those who are lost.

Discussion #2

1. How might you cooperate with the Lord to reach the "whoevers" in your life with the message of love and salvation? What specific actions could you take to draw closer to them this week? (Take an extended time for this question, as it is the main application of this passage.)

    Everyday life
    Step out of the box – comfort zone &
    help others.

2. Why do you think that we often run away from God's throne when we sin? Based on the love of God we learn about in John 3:16–21, which way should we run when we sin? Which way do you normally run in tough times?

3. God is interested in the world (John 3:16). Is your tendency to be interested in yourself or in the needs that exist in the world? Can you name specific actions in your life that show one or the other to be true?

    By pass your needs & help some one else.
    Reach out to who so evers –

4. Take some time to pray as you end the study.

PERSONAL REFLECTION

Day One

1. Read John 3:1–21.

2. Not even Nicodemus, a very prominent member of the Jewish faith, automatically gained entrance into God's kingdom. What does it take for someone today to have eternal life in God's kingdom? Is "growing up in the church" enough?

3. Do you think that most Christians today really believe that those who do not have faith in Jesus are lost for an eternity? If we really believed that it is true, how would this change our lives, our churches, and our ministries?

4. Begin to memorize the key verse for this passage: John 3:16.

Day Two

1. Read Ezekiel 36:16–27.

2. Jesus says in John 3:5 that the only way to enter the kingdom of God is to be "born of water and the Spirit." Ezekiel 36:16–27 is one of the most important background passages for understanding the meaning of the phrase, "born of water and the Spirit." Meditate on this once more, noting the changes that will happen when the Spirit comes upon people, namely, obedience that brings glory to God. How do you see this kind of obedience at work in your life? If you don't see it, what might be stopping you from exercising that obedience?

3. Nicodemus did not fully understand Jesus, perhaps because he did not understand the Old Testament prophecies about the Messiah. Why might it be important for us today to spend time reading the Bible so that we better understand Jesus?

Day Three

1. Read Ephesians 2:1–10.

2. Do you sometimes think that people are beyond the reach of God? That they are too "dead in their sins" to be "made alive in Christ" or "born again"? Have you given up on anyone? Have you yourself ever felt too far gone to be saved?

3. Remember that there is a spiritual battle in evangelism. It is not just about truth claims; people need to respond in faith. Spend some time praying for the evangelistic encounters that you will have this week, asking the Lord to strengthen you in the battle, and limit the influence of the evil one as you share the gospel.

Day Four

1. Read Colossians 2:15 and 1 Peter 5:8.

2. Ask the Lord to show you how you can bring his life-giving message to those around you. Think about who the "whoevers" are in your life that God might be seeking. Ask God to reveal five people to you. Try to come up with a list of specific actions that you could take to reach your friends, family, neighbors, and even those on the other side of the world with the good news of Jesus.

3. Do you think that you love people the way that God loves in this passage? John 3 says that true love acts, sends, and gives. In what ways are you giving or sacrificing for those around you?

Day Five

1. Read John 3:1–21 one more time.

2. Pray through the entire passage verse by verse, allowing the deeper meaning that you have discovered lead you as you pray. Ask the Spirit to continue to remind you of what you have learned and to help you apply these truths to your life. Jot down any further applications that come to mind as you pray.

3. Turn back to the discussion questions from the video teaching (Discussion #1, #2). If there are questions that your group did not have time to discuss or questions that you might like to think more about, use this time to review and reflect further.

CALLED TO RESTORATION
Samaritan Woman

◇

DR. MATT WILLIAMS

JOHN 4:4–26

*Whoever drinks the water I give them will never thirst.
Indeed, the water I give them will become in them a
spring of water welling up to eternal life.*

John 4:14

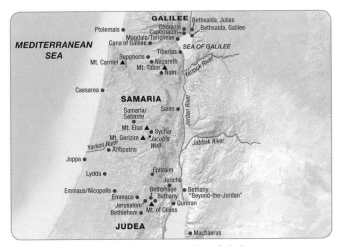

Location of Passage: Jacob's Well, Sychar

PART 1: DIGGING FOR MEANING

The Savior of the world restored this shame-filled Samaritan woman from a misfit to an honored VIP.

Video Introduction by Bruce Marchiano
Video Scripture Reading: John 4:4–26

◆ Words hurt.

◆ Samaritan woman had three strikes.

Somantain — Women — Sinner

unclean-sinful   not to talk   busy w/ men
foreigners   to women   5 husbands
Outsider   always unclean shameful
             2nd Class   damaged goods

◆ Samaritan woman vs. Nicodemus

poor + sinner   rich.
foreigner
rejected

◆ 1. First strike, she was a Samaritan.

Lived in neglect + loneliness
Jesus asked her for a water

◆ Samaritan=foreigner

> ### Did You Know?
>
> Jews in Jesus's day viewed the Samaritans not only as the children of political rebels but as racial half-breeds whose religion was tainted by various unacceptable elements.[17]

◆ But Jesus spoke with . . .

Jesus wants to restore her.
Living water for Spiritual

◆ Second strike, she was a woman.

She finds forgiveness —
Leaves her water jar setting by the well
Jesus offers her eternal life
Jesus took away the sexual change.
She introduce the Savior to the town

◆ But Jesus spoke with . . .

> ## Did You Know?
>
> Jewish people in Jesus's day called Samaritan women "menstruates from the cradle."[18] One ancient rabbinic teaching says: "Do not talk much with women. This was said about one's own wife; how much more so about the wife of one's neighbor. Therefore, the sages have said: He who talks too much with women brings evil upon himself and neglects the study of the Torah and will in the end inherit Gehenna."[19]

◆ 3. Third strike, the Samaritan woman was a sinner.

She was given a new life.

> ## Did You Know?
>
> Rabbinic opinion disapproved more than three marriages, even though they were legally permissible.[20]

◆ Sexual purity and honor in the first century

◆ But Jesus spoke with . . .

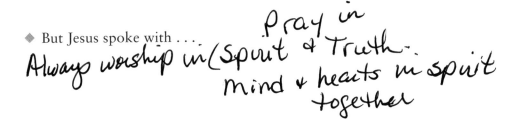

Pray in

Always worship in (Spirit & Truth -.
mind & hearts in spirit
together

◆ The outskirts of society . . . rejected

◆ But Jesus . . .

Jacob's Well, circa 1910

"The surprising thing is not that Jesus has asked her for help with a drink of water. It is that he would ask her for anything. . . . They should have no contact."

—Gary Burge[21]

Jesus restores her in four ways:

◆ 1. Jesus offers her living water.

> *If you knew the gift of God and who it is that asks you for a drink, you would have asked him and he would have given you living water.*
>
> John 4:10

> "It was 'living water' that took away defilement and made acceptable worshipers out of unclean people."
>
> —Leon Morris[22]

◆ 2. Jesus offers her eternal life.

> *Whoever drinks the water I give them will never thirst. Indeed, the water I give them will become in them a spring of water welling up to eternal life.*
>
> John 4:14

◇ Eternal life has two different ideas: quantity and quality

> *"It is about cleansing—and restoration. . . . To offer a stranger a drink of water might be a gesture of hospitality and friendship. To suggest she needs living water is something different; it is prophetic."*
>
> —Gary Burge[23]

◆ 3. Jesus offers her honor.

◇ Who introduced you to Jesus?

◆ 4. Jesus offers her a new way to worship God.

God is spirit, and his worshipers must worship in the Spirit and in truth.

John 4:24

◇ "In the Spirit and in truth" is a single idea.

"John's 'worship in the Spirit' is a foretaste of the eschatological worship around God's throne depicted in Revelation."

—Craig Keener[24]

◆ The "rejected Samaritan woman" was restored by the Savior of the world.

I lay a stone in Zion, a chosen and precious cornerstone, and the one who trusts in him will never be put to shame.

1 Peter 2:6

◆ What about you?

Discussion #1

1. Based on the background information discussed in the video, what makes it surprising that Jesus spoke to the Samaritan woman (John 4:9)? If you were one of the disciples, would you have been surprised that Jesus spoke to her (John 4:27)? *- yes, but Jesus surpris-*

Wasn't done back then. than with stuff all the time. Men didn't speak to women. Considered a foreigner, sinner & unclean women.

2. If you were the Samaritan woman, with three strikes, how would it change your life if Jesus really could provide "living water," or cleansing for you? Be specific: think spiritually, but also socially, relationally, etc.

Would lift a burden off your shoulders, to have This man talk to you. She went at noontime - when others wouldn't be going.

3. If you know Christ, who introduced you to Jesus? How much honor do they hold in your life? How was your life changed by meeting Jesus?

I grew up in a church -

4. Do most people that you know worship God in "spirittruth" or do they emphasize either the Spirit *or* truth in their worship? What does it look like when one is emphasized over the other? How can we include both ideas in our worship?

We need to allow the spirit truth to rain over us - Let the Holy Spirit guide you through it all.

PART 2: YOUR LIFE TODAY

If Jesus restored the Samaritan woman—someone with three strikes—he can restore us!

◆ Feeling like we are second class

Not good enough to pray to Jesus - Transformed

◆ Good news

> The Samaritan woman "knows that she has been living in isolation not only from her community but from God."
>
> —Gary Burge[25]

◆ We do not deserve God's goodness.

Our Lord loves to restore us & gives us Praise + honor.

◆ Restored

◆ A calling/purpose

Listen for his voice

3 strikes

> "Her testimony results in the belief of many other Samaritans, who are enabled to encounter Jesus for themselves."
>
> —Andrew Lincoln[26]

◆ Jesus restores people today. *Like your GPS —*

He erases our past.
you may have made a few
wrong turns in your life
But Jesus is saying Re calculating

◆ What are your three strikes?

◆ Etch A Sketch and GPS—recalculating

Discussion #2

1. Discuss the value of women in first-century culture compared to the value that Jesus showed the Samaritan woman. How can we show more value to women in our culture, and in your own circles of influence?

Women were to wear dresses / Not pants-

2. Think about all of the social and racial barriers that Jesus crossed in order to minister to the Samaritan woman. What are the social and racial barriers you see in churches today? What would it look like if we ministered to *all* people without those barriers?

3. The woman left her water jar because she found higher value in Jesus. What have you left for Jesus? Is there still something that you are clinging to that you need to leave behind?

4. Think about the shame/guilt that you carry. What are your three strikes? Pray through John 4:5–26. In your mind's eye "watch" Jesus's interaction with the Samaritan woman, remembering the cultural and religious significance of her three strikes. Now, place yourself there at the well and pray to Jesus. Tell him about your three strikes. Ask him for forgiveness and cleansing. Don't be in a hurry; take time to sit with Jesus at the well.

PERSONAL REFLECTION

Day One

1. Read Zephaniah 3:14–20.

2. Take some time to journal what the Lord showed you in the prayer and discussion time during the group study (especially through Discussion #2, question 4).

3. Begin to memorize the key verse for this passage: John 4:14.

Day Two

1. Read Psalm 42:1–5.

2. Jesus offered the Samaritan woman over two thousand years ago living water to quench her thirst. There is only *one* source that can eternally and sufficiently quench your thirst. Are you thirsty for Jesus's living water?

3. Pray through your priorities. Is Jesus your number one priority? Be honest in your prayer time. What are the dry areas in your life that need Jesus's living water? How can you make him a higher focus in your life? Any specific ideas?

Day Three

1. Read John 4:4–26.

2. Do you sometimes feel like an outsider? Spend some time in prayer, allowing Jesus to show you that he cares for you and wants to honor you, just as he did for the Samaritan woman.

3. Now, reflect on those in your community who might feel like outsiders. Jesus broke down racial and social barriers in order to reach the Samaritan woman with the good news. What specific things could you do in your community to reach those who might feel like outsiders?

Day Four

1. Read John 4:23, 39–42 and 20:21.

2. John 4:23 says that God "seeks" worshipers. God is active and takes the initiative in seeking people for salvation. Take some time to think about your role in extending salvation to your "neighbors."

3. Now take some time to reflect what your role is in extending salvation to the entire world. You may not be sent to go as a missionary, but we are all called to extend salvation to the utmost parts of the world, as well as be missional in our immediate worlds. How can you help support those who are called to go—financially, emotionally, and prayerfully? Be specific in your ideas. Try to come up with an action plan that you could put into practice.

Day Five

1. Read John 4:4–26 one more time.

2. Pray through the entire passage verse by verse, allowing the deeper meaning that you have discovered lead you as you pray. Ask the Spirit to continue to remind you of what you have learned and to help you apply these truths to your life. Jot down any further applications that come to mind as you pray.

3. Turn back to the discussion questions from the video teaching (Discussion #1, #2). If there are questions that your group did not have time to discuss or questions that you might like to think more about, use this time to review and reflect further.

CALLED TO HEALING WORK
Healing the Paralytic

———◇———

DR. MARK STRAUSS

JOHN 5:1–18

*Then Jesus said to him, "Get up! Pick up your
mat and walk." At once the man was cured;
he picked up his mat and walked. The day
on which this took place was a Sabbath.*

John 5:8–9

Ruins of the Pools of Bethesda, northern pool
Location of Passage: Pool of Bethesda, Jerusalem

PART 1: DIGGING FOR MEANING

Jesus heals a paralytic who uses his miraculous ability to walk away from Jesus. It's an astoundingly ironic and sad story.

We could have given this message the title *Keeping the Lights on during Sabbath* because in this passage Jesus makes one of the most profound statements in Scripture. When accused of working on the Sabbath, he basically says, "Hey, God the Father works on the Sabbath . . . and, by the way, so do I." A remarkable claim to be equal with the Father!

Video Introduction by Bruce Marchiano
Video Scripture Reading: John 5:1–18

◆ Working on holidays

7-11's, Police,
Jesus it always on Duty

◆ The purpose of signs is (1) to reveal Jesus's glory and (2) to provoke faith.

◆ Context: Jewish festivals

Feast of Tabernacles.
Jesus attends all Festivals

◆ Pool of Bethesda

In Jerusalem
Sheep Gate -
temple sacrifices
James 5:3

Model of the Pools of Bethesda

72

◆ There is a man at the pool who had been an invalid for thirty-eight years.

[handwritten note:] V verse 4 - Angels came down went to the pool to be healed "Do you want to be healed?" Seeking to provoke faith. He has a magical No one to help - All he has to do + ask Jesus. Jesus heals the man ~

> When Jesus saw him lying there and learned that he had been in this condition for a long time, he asked him, "Do you want to get well?"
>
> John 5:6

◆ Faith or excuses?

◆ Problems with the man's statement:

◇ Magical view of healing

◇ "No one to help"

Then the lame would leap like a deer.

Isaiah 35:6

> *"In the Old Testament, the leaping of lame men is sometimes associated with the end time when the Messiah would come (e.g. Isaiah 35:6)."*
>
> —Leon Morris[29]

◆ Jesus heals the man.

◆ Sabbath healing and work according to the Jewish law.

◆ The Jewish leaders accuse the man of working on the Sabbath.

Did You Know?

The Hebrew word *shabbat* comes from the Hebrew verb *shabat*, which literally means "to cease." Although "Sabbath" is almost universally translated as "rest" or a "period of rest", a more literal translation would be "ceasing", with the implication of "ceasing from work." [30]

> *And so the Jewish leaders said to the man who had been healed, "It is the Sabbath; the law forbids you to carry your mat." But he replied, "The man who made me well said to me, 'Pick up your mat and walk.'"*
>
> John 5:10–11

◆ Shocking response of the leaders

◆ Jesus finds the man again.

> *Later Jesus found him at the temple and said to him, "See, you are well again. Stop sinning or something worse may happen to you."*
>
> John 5:14

◆ Can sickness be caused by sin?

◆ Is all sickness caused by sin?

◆ What is worse than physical suffering?

◆ The healed man reports Jesus to the Jewish authorities.

◆ The healing provokes persecution.

◆ Accusation of a Sabbath violation

> "Although God works constantly, he cannot rightly be charged with violating the Sabbath law, since the entire universe is his domain (Is. 6:3), and therefore he never carries anything outside it ["Do not bring a load out of your houses or do any work on the Sabbath, but keep the Sabbath day holy, as I commanded your ancestors." Jeremiah 17:22] (Exodus Rabbah 30:9)."
>
> —D. A. Carson[31]

> In his defense Jesus said to them, "My Father is always at his work to this very day, and I too am working." For this reason they tried all the more to kill him; not only was he breaking the Sabbath, but he was even calling God his own Father, making himself equal with God.
>
> John 5:17–18

◆ Jesus places himself in the same position as God!

◆ Signs reveal Jesus's glory.

◆ Signs provoke faith.

Discussion #1

1. It seems that the man had a "magical" view of the healing waters.
Do you ever feel like God will answer your prayers if you are good
enough or pray long enough? Why or why not?

Don't give up & continue praying

2. What makes it difficult to believe that God heals people today?

It's not difficult –
People wants to actually see it.
Evanjalism –
where is your God now – that makes it difficult

3. Does it surprise you that the man did not thank or worship Jesus
after the healing? Imagine for a moment that you are the man in
John 5 who cannot walk. What significance would the miracle
mean for you if you were healed in order to walk after thirty-eight
years? How would you react to Jesus healing you? Be specific.

yes

Couldn't stop talking about it – (hadn't walked
in 38 yrs.) He was a dependet person –
↗ Rejoice –

4. Does it make sense to you that the Jewish leaders wanted to
persecute Jesus for healing on the Sabbath? Why or why not?
What do you think the persecution tells us about their hearts and
their devotion for God? (Consider what Jesus said about them in
John 5:42.)

they don't his from the line of David –
can't figure out how the Son of a carpinter doing all these
meraculis things.
Trusting in God alone

PART 2: YOUR LIFE TODAY

Our identity as healed Christians calls us to bring healing to a hurting world. We are God's ambassadors for a lost world, sharing with them that the God of grace wants to heal them too.

◈ Five applications:

◇ 1. We are called to live lives of trust and dependence on God.

> "God made you, but you rebelled against him. Instead of punishing you, he put in motion a plan to rescue you. . . . He sent his Son to die so that you'd throw yourself at his feet and ask him to rescue you."
>
> —Matt Carter and Josh Wredberg[32]

◇ 2. We can have confidence that when we ask, God can and will meet our needs.

Can meet our needs: transcendence

ilistrate 2   Soverghty

Will meet our needs: immanence

Presents of God.
Meets our needs -
Soverthy + His Grace -

Establish priority's in God

on't make excuses - take responsibility for our actions

79

◇ 3. God desires us to take responsibility for our actions.

◇ 4. Remember what is important and establish priorities.

Seek first the kingdom of God and his righteousness and all these other things will be given to you as well.

Matthew 6:33

◇ 5. Our response should be (1) gratitude and (2) extending God's grace to others.

Recipe for success in life:
prays God daily
offer others what we have been
freely given.
We have been embassodors.

Discussion #2

1. Mark Strauss says that we need to get our priorities right. Is there anything that you desire more than you desire God? Do you have any ideas on how you can surrender these other desires to the Lord?

2. Do you doubt that God *can* meet your needs? Do you doubt that he *will* meet your needs? Have you ever been disappointed because you thought that God would do something for you, but then he did not do it? Does it help you to remember that Jesus also suffered during his lifetime?

3. Mark Strauss said that we should respond to God in our life by having an attitude of gratitude and by becoming agents of reconciliation, sharing God with others. What can you thank God for? Who would make your list of people who could benefit from you sharing God's work in your life? Can you think of specific ways that would allow you to spend time with them, seeking opportunities to share more deeply about your God-story?

    live our lives as an example -

4. Take some time to pray as you end the study, asking God to help you to trust him fully, even in moments of despair and disappointment with him.

PERSONAL REFLECTION

Day One

1. Read John 5:1–15.

2. Focus today on Mark Strauss's first application: "We are called to live lives of trust and dependence on God." Read Matthew 7:7–11, and then pray through all the things for which you must rely upon God: life, health, peace, joy, family, friends, ministry, etc.

3. Are there areas of your life where you are not trusting or depending upon God? If so, take some time to pray through those, asking God to heal and help you.

4. Begin to memorize the key verses for this passage: John 5:8–9.

Day Two

1. Read John 5:16–30.

2. Focus today on Mark Strauss's second application: "We can have confidence that when we ask, God *can* and *will* meet our needs." Reflect on both the transcendence and immanence of God. Which of those seems more real to you: that God is beyond, or that he is near? Brother Lawrence used to "Practice the Presence of God" everywhere that he went, no matter what he was doing. How could you do this in your life?

3. Perhaps one of the most difficult aspects of life is that God doesn't always *feel* present to us, and he doesn't always do what we want him to do. Are there areas of your life that you wish God would act, but he doesn't? Think back over your life and thank God for all the good things that he *has* done for you.

Day Three

1. Read John 4:43–54. (Note that unlike in John 5, the royal official believed Jesus's word and responded correctly.)

2. Focus today on Mark Strauss's third application: "God desires us to take responsibility for our actions." Is there unconfessed sin in your life? Confess it now and claim the truth of 1 John 1:9.

3. The Lord is quick to forgive and to remove our sin so we can be reconciled to him. But what about other people? Are there people in your life against whom you bear a grudge or unforgiveness? Spend time in prayer, asking the Spirit to bring to mind anyone whom you have not forgiven, remembering the truth of Colossians 3:13. Then ask the Lord how you can make these things right.

Day Four

1. Read and meditate on 2 Corinthians 5:20.

2. Focus today on Mark Strauss's final application: "We need to offer to others what we have been freely given." Have you thought much about your role in reaching the world? Read Romans 10:14, then ask the Lord to bring to mind three names of people whom you could reach with the gospel message.

3. We not only play a role in reaching those close to us with the gospel message, but also are instrumental in reaching the entire world. Ask the Lord to show you one or two specific ministries that you could prayerfully or financially support that bring the gospel message to the needy throughout the world.

4. In the first-century Jewish world, paralytics were on the outskirts of the community. They were socially expendable. In our world, who are those on the outskirts of society and seen as expendable? Just as Jesus noticed the paralytic in John 5 and went to heal him, we today are called to notice those who are on the outskirts of society, and attempt to help them. Do you see them? Are they on your radar? How are you trying to reach them?

Day Five

1. Read John 5:1–18 one more time.

2. Pray through the entire passage verse by verse, allowing the deeper meaning that you have discovered lead you as you pray. Ask the Spirit to continue to remind you of what you have learned and to help you apply these truths to your life. Jot down any further applications that come to mind as you pray.

3. Turn back to the discussion questions from the video teaching (Discussion #1, #2). If there are questions that your group did not have time to discuss or questions that you might like to think about more deeply, use this time to review and reflect further. Pray a thanksgiving prayer that Jesus has healed, and then pray that you might be an instrument of God's healing to those whom you know.

CALLED TO BE A TEMPLE
If You Are Thirsty

◇

DR. MATT WILLIAMS

JOHN 7:37–44

*On the last and greatest day of the festival, Jesus stood
and said in a loud voice, "Let anyone who is thirsty come
to me and drink. Whoever believes in me, as Scripture
has said, rivers of living water will flow from within them."*

John 7:37–38

Location of Passage: Temple Courts, Jerusalem

PART 1: DIGGING FOR MEANING

We who believe in Jesus become temples and will impact those around us through the life-giving power of the Spirit flowing out of us.

Video Introduction by Bruce Marchiano
Video Scripture Reading: John 7:37–44

◆ Feast of Tabernacles

Let anyone who is thirsty come to me —
We are the temples of the Holy Spirit

◆ Mornings at the Feast of Tabernacles: Water

Preast go down from temple fill a golden vase of water + go back up to temple
Every morning of the feast

◆ Jesus teaches in the temple courts.

> **Did You Know?**
>
> The celebration was known as the Feast of Tents or Booths since the participants in the festival camped out in homemade shelters of leafy branches erected on rooftops or in fields.[33]

Stairs down to the Pool of Siloam

> *On the last and greatest day of the festival, Jesus stood and said in a loud voice, "Let anyone who is thirsty come to me and drink. Whoever believes in me, as Scripture has said, rivers of living water will flow from within them."*
>
> John 7:37–38

◆ What is Jesus saying?

John 7:37b-38
Thirsty looking for water? I got it—
I can more than satisfy you thirst.

> "Those seeking eschatological water need to look no further.
> ... Jesus is the source for what Tabernacles seeks."
>
> —Gary Burge[34]

◆ What does Jesus mean by "living water"?

Spiritual Cleansing for those who believe in him.

◆ A deeper meaning: Ezekiel 47

◆ A little deeper summary of Ezekiel 47

Water will flow out of Jerusalem
transformed into clean water
trees will grow in abundance
+ the trees will bare fruit—

◆ En Gedi, on the shore of the Dead Sea

Salt on this rock

This fruit will kill you

| En Gedi shoreline | Salt on rocks in the Dead Sea | Sodom's Apple fruit |

◆ So, what is this living water?

Spirit who those who believe in Jesus —

> "Whoever believes in me, as Scripture has said, rivers of living water will flow from within them." By this he meant the Spirit, whom those who believed in him were later to receive.
>
> John 7:37–39a

◆ What does the temple mentioned in Ezekiel have to do with us Christians?

We are temples — + water that flows out of us are the Holy spirits.

Don't you know that you yourselves are God's temple and that God's Spirit dwells in your midst?

1 Corinthians 3:16

◆ Who are you?

Holy temple of God -
Spirit flows out of us
to bring life -

"When Jesus offered the Samaritan woman living water, he said it would become in her 'a spring of water welling up to eternal life' (4:13–14), which is not that much different from saying that 'rivers of living water will flow from within them.'"

—Colin Kruse[35]

◆ Let's put all of this together:

Jesus brings spiritual freedom from sins

◆ You are a temple.

Living water flows out of us to bring
life.
We influence everyone that we come in
contact with.

89

◆ Result of Jesus's teaching

> *On hearing his words, some of the people said, "Surely this man is the Prophet." Others said, "He is the Messiah." Still others asked, "How can the Messiah come from Galilee? Does not Scripture say that the Messiah will come from David's descendants and from Bethlehem, the town where David lived?" Thus, the people were divided because of Jesus.*
>
> John 7:40–43

◆ Jesus was fulfilling Old Testament prophecies in unexpected ways.

Filling them in very unexpected way – Jesus brings spiritual life. Those who believe in Jesus will become Temples –

◆ People today are still divided about Jesus.

Discussion #1

1. Why do you think Jesus called people at the Feast of Tabernacles to come to him if they were thirsty? (Relate it to the morning activities at the feast.)

Spiritual cleansing;
food had been provided

2. Take some time as a group to reflect on Ezekiel 47. What does it mean? How do you think Jesus fulfills that passage?

Dry bones coming back + restore
Water that flows out of water
Died Sea remains dead—there's no
life from it —

3. If all Christians today saw themselves as *temples*, how would that change the way they live?

We have this amazing live to this
dead world.

4. People today are still divided about Jesus. How have people in your own life responded to Jesus? Many think that Jesus will make their life all better and take away all their problems, but that doesn't always happen. How could you show them who Jesus really is?

PART 2: YOUR LIFE TODAY

Wherever I go, I am a temple; and the Spirit is flowing out of me, impacting every single person with whom I come into contact.

◆ We are temples of God's Spirit.

◆ The significance of this

◆ The *Holy* Spirit resides within us.

 ◇ Justification

 ◇ Sanctification

> "The final and perfect manifestation of God was in Jesus, whose ministry would result in God's dwelling neither in a tent nor in a temple, but in people's hearts by his Spirit."
>
> —Leon Morris[36]

◆ How does Jesus cleanse us?

If we confess our sins, he is faithful and just and will forgive us our sins and purify us from all unrighteousness.

1 John 1:9

◆ We need to remember . . .

◆ The Holy Spirit also impacts all those around us.

◆ God has called us to impact those around us.

◆ Who are we?

◆ What is our purpose?

> "Jesus calls people out of the world and into the faith community, then sends them into the world . . . in order to call others to faith."
>
> —Craig Koester[37]

◆ Our "Dead Sea"

◆ My secret identity

◆ Who are you?

> "Believers are not self-centered. . . . When people believe they become servants of God and God uses them to be the means of bringing blessing to others."
>
> —Leon Morris[38]

Called to Be a Temple

Discussion #2

1. Christians are called temples because the Holy Spirit resides in us. What impact does recognizing this truth have on your life?

   purpose
   diretion

2. God's Spirit not only lives in us but flows out of us to impact all the nations, bringing cleansing, life, abundant fruit, and healing to even the deadest of places. How have you impacted those around you with *life*? Would you say that your own life could be described as the Spirit flowing out of you like a river?

3. Think of one person that you know who is struggling. If God allowed you to be the conduit of the Spirit in their life, how would their life change? Do you have any ideas of specific things that you can do this week to try to make this happen?

   Bring hope + joy to this world
   peace

4. Spend some time in prayer. Imagine yourself at a river (a metaphor for the Holy Spirit in John 7:38–39). Allow the Spirit to cleanse you of all of your sin and shame—washing you clean. Then, imagine walking away from the river as a cleansed temple of God, carrying the Lord's glory with you as a bearer of the Holy Spirit. Imagine walking with Jesus throughout your day. The Lord has chosen you and given you his Spirit. You are the temple of the holy God. He resides within you and wants to flow out of you to impact *everyone* whom you will contact today. Enjoy the journey! Let the river flow!

95

PERSONAL REFLECTION

Day One

1. Read Ezekiel 47.

2. Take some extended time to pray through the last discussion question of the video study (Discussion #2, question 4). Think through different areas of your life, imagining how the Spirit might work through you to minister to others.

3. If you wore a "Temple Woman/Man" T-shirt to remind you of your secret identity as a temple of God, what impact might that have on you this week as you interact with other people? If not a T-shirt, what is something that could consistently remind you of your identity as a temple of God?

4. Begin to memorize the key verses for this passage: John 7:37–38.

Day Two

1. Read John 15:1–8.

2. From John 15, we learn that we are already clean. Do you feel cleansed? Some struggle to believe that they are truly clean because of sins that they have committed in the past or sins that others have committed against them. If you struggle, it might be helpful to find a mentor that can walk through your sin, shame, and guilt with you. Spend some time asking the Lord to bring to mind someone who might mentor you.

3. Do you think that it is possible to squelch the flow of the Spirit in your life? Have you ever done that? Ask the Lord in prayer to show you if there is there anything in your life that might be unconsciously squelching the flow of the Spirit—habits, addictions, relationships, etc.

4. From John 15, we learn that the only way to bear fruit is to stay connected to Jesus, to remain in him. What does it mean to "remain in Jesus"? Can you list specific actions that you can take to stay closer to Jesus this week? (Don't forget the classic spiritual formation practices: prayer, Bible reading, meditation, fellowship, ministry, fasting, journaling, worship, etc.)

Day Three

1. Read John 15:16–21.

2. As we allow the Spirit to flow out of us to impact the world, the response will not always be positive, as we read in John 15. Have you had negative ministry experiences? If so, how have they impacted your ministry in the present?

3. Pray through possible ways that you could better participate with the Spirit flowing out of your life to affect others. Think of specific people in your life. Write down some ideas the Lord gives you about how to minister to them.

Day Four

1. Read Revelation 22:1–2.

2. Notice that the same idea in Ezekiel 47 is found in the very last chapter of the Bible: the river brings life—yielding fruit and bring healing "to the nations." *Life* in the gospel of John means both quality of life in the present (joy, forgiveness, peace, love, etc.) as well as a quantity of life (for all eternity). If you opened a business and were able to sell people the life that the Bible talks about, how much would it be worth?

3. Given that people all around us are struggling, what do you think keeps us from spending more time sharing this good news of life with them? Pray through the priorities that you presently have in your life. Ask the Lord to show you if you need to make any changes in order to prioritize living this life and sharing it with others.

Day Five

1. Read John 7:37–44 one more time.

2. Pray through the entire passage verse by verse, allowing the deeper meaning that you have discovered lead you as you pray. Ask the Spirit to continue to remind you of what you have learned and to help you apply these truths to your life. Jot down any further applications that come to mind as you pray.

3. Turn back to the discussion questions from the video teaching (Discussion #1, #2). If there are questions that your group did not have time to discuss or questions that you might like to think more about, use this time to review and reflect further.

CALLED TO BE A LIGHT
I Am the Light of the World

◇

DR. JEREMY TREAT

JOHN 8:12

When Jesus spoke again to the people, he said, "I am the light of the world. Whoever follows me will never walk in darkness, but will have the light of life."

John 8:12

Court of the Women (Treasury)
Location of Passage: Temple Courts, Jerusalem,
near where offerings are put (John 8:20).

PART 1: DIGGING FOR MEANING

Jesus is claiming to be God, the Messiah, who is bringing life to anyone in the world who will believe and follow him.

Video Introduction by Bruce Marchiano
Video Scripture Reading: John 8:12

◆ Light has a powerful impact on life.

The Lord is my light + my Salvation Jesus is the light of the world to claim truth –

◆ Darkness

The people walking in the darkness has seen light Isiah 9: 2, 6-7a   Darkness can be depressing.

◆ In a world darkened by sin, Jesus proclaims . . .

You will know the truth & the truth will set you free.

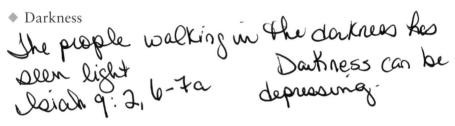

> I am the light of the world. Whoever follows me will never walk in darkness, but will have the light of life.
>
> John 8:12

◆ First-century context

who so ever committeth sin is the servant of sin John 8: 34

> *"Four huge lamps in the temple's court of women [were lit].
> . . . 'Men of piety and good works' danced through the night,
> holding burning torches in their hands and singing songs
> and praises. . . . The light from the temple area shedding its
> glow all over Jerusalem. In this context Jesus declares to the
> people, I am the light of the world."*
>
> —D. A. Carson[39]

◆ Light is about revelation.

◆ 1. Jesus is the Light that proclaims Truth.

Then you will know the truth, and the truth will set you free.

John 8:32

◇ Jesus is the Truth (John 14:6).

I'm the truth
I'm the Shephard
I'm the Gate

◆ 2. Jesus is the Light that liberates captives.

> **Did You Know?**
>
> The Israelites were trained to sing, "The Lord is my light and my salvation" (Psalm 27:1).[40]

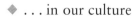

Very truly I tell you, everyone who sins is a slave to sin. Now a slave has no permanent place in the family, but a son belongs to it forever. So if the Son sets you free, you will be free indeed.

John 8:34–36

◆ Freedom means . . .

◆ . . . in our culture

◆ . . . in Jesus's teaching

◆ Exodus story *John 8:44*

you are your father the devil & the lusts of
your father ye will do.
The devil is real God is the light

◆ . . . freedom from

◆ . . . freedom for

◆ 3. Jesus is the Light that conquers evil.

> *You belong to your father, the devil, and you want to carry*
> *out your father's desires. He was a murderer from the*
> *beginning, not holding to the truth, for there is no truth in*
> *him. When he lies, he speaks his native language, for he is*
> *a liar and the father of lies.*
>
> John 8:44

◆ A cosmic battle

Did You Know?

Jewish texts call the devil Mastema, which can mean enmity, one who accuses, disturbs, hates, or persecutes.[41]

◆ *We* are in a battle.

◆ Jesus claims authority and power.

So Jesus said, "When you have lifted up the Son of Man, then you will know that I am he."

John 8:28a

◆ "Lifted up" means . . .

"Each time the 'lifting up' of Jesus on the cross is mentioned in this Gospel, something good comes of it."

—J. Ramsey Michaels[42]

◆ Jesus makes a bold claim: "I am."

> "Although the title 'light' or 'lamp of the world' applied to various figures, only God or his Wisdom/Torah would publicly make the claim for himself."
>
> —Craig Keener[43]

◆ Exodus 3

> Moses said to God, "Suppose I go to the Israelites and say to them, 'The God of your fathers has sent me to you,' and they ask me, 'What is his name?' Then what shall I tell them?" God said to Moses, "I AM WHO I AM."
>
> Exodus 3:13–14a

◆ Jesus claims to be God.

Discussion #1

1. What is the relationship between light and truth? In our world today, many claim that there is no such thing as truth. Do you think that an ultimate truth exists? What difference does it make? How can we show the world that an ultimate Truth exists?

   Jesus is the light of the world & claim the truth.

2. Jeremy Treat said that Jesus is the Light that liberates captives. If this is true, why do you think that many Christians today continue to live in some kind of bondage—whether literal bondage or bondage to sin patterns, anxiety, depression, health issues, etc.? Do you believe that the light of Jesus is powerful enough to reach into the darkness of your life and deliver you?

   It is but some people just won't let it in - Not excepting Repititive over & over that they just won't let Jesus in.

3. Jeremy Treat also said that Jesus is the Light that conquers evil. Do you think that a cosmic battle exists? How have you seen evidence of it in your own life?

   yes↑

   Kids with social media - If kids believe in Christ they have a good start - Reality -

4. Does the exposing light of Jesus give you joy that you are now able to see the Truth, or does it produce fear and shame for what it exposes?

   where their life stands in regards to Jesus.

PART 2: YOUR LIFE TODAY

When Jesus says, "I am the light of the world," he makes a powerful statement about who he is, but what he says is also life-changing for us.

◆ Jesus's teachings change us.

> Whoever follows me will never walk in darkness, but will have the light of life.
>
> John 8:12b

◆ Artificial light

◆ Man-made religion

> To the Jews who had believed him, Jesus said, "If you hold to my teaching, you are really my disciples."
>
> John 8:31

◆ Walk in the Light—knowing and following Jesus by:

◇ Bring our sin into the Light. - *Confession*

This is the message we have heard from him and declare to you: God is light; in him there is no darkness at all. If we claim to have fellowship with him and yet walk in the darkness, we lie and do not live out the truth. But if we walk in the light, as he is in the light, we have fellowship with one another, and the blood of Jesus, his Son, purifies us from all sin. If we claim to be without sin, we deceive ourselves and the truth is not in us. If we confess our sins, he is faithful and just and will forgive us our sins and purify us from all unrighteousness.

1 John 1:5–9

◆ What is confession?

A path to freedom we are washed clean & are forgiven. Healing

◇ Rejoice in God's grace.

His the light of the world Goodnews about God's free grace in God

"The only sin that will keep a grip on you is the sin that you keep in the dark."

— Jeremy Treat

◆ What does *gospel* mean?

◆ Guilt/shame vs. gospel/gratitude motivation

◆ Be the Light.

Its dwelling in you by faith.
Let your light shine -
Light brings life -

We need water &
light to grow

> You are the light of the world. A town built on a hill cannot be hidden. Neither do people light a lamp and put it under a bowl. Instead they put it on its stand, and it gives light to everyone in the house. In the same way, let your light shine before others, that they may see your good deeds and glorify your Father in heaven.
>
> Matthew 5:14–16

> "If Jesus is the light, walking 'in the light' is a description of discipleship."
>
> —Gary Burge[44]

◆ Light brings life.

We need to stay in the light
By:
Bible Study
Fellowship with others.
Prayer

Discussion #2

1. In John 8:31, Jesus said, "If you hold to my teaching, you are really my disciples." Do you think that obedience is necessary for Christians? Do most Christians believe this is true? What evidence have you seen for or against this belief?

2. Jeremy Treat said, "The only sin that will keep a grip on you is the sin that you keep in the dark." Do you think that sin loses its power when it is brought into the light? Why do you think Christians do not want their sins to be brought into the light?

3. Our purpose according to this passage is to be the light to the world. What does that look like in your life? If you really followed this idea, what would it look like?

4. Jeremy Treat says that we need water and light. What specific actions can we take to place ourselves "on the window sill" so that God's water and light impacts us and brings abundant life so that we can grow and flourish to the glory of God?

5. Take some time to pray as you end the study.

PERSONAL REFLECTION

Day One

1. Read John 8:12.

2. Pray and thank God that he is the light who reveals truth and dispels darkness.

3. Are there sins that are hiding in your life presently that you do not talk to Jesus about? What areas of your life remain in darkness? What would look different if they were in the light? Confess these things to the Lord in prayer.

4. Are there any lies that you believe about God's character because of past experiences? Ask the Lord to begin to reveal the truth about his character and heal those areas of hurt.

5. Begin to memorize the key verse for this passage: John 8:12.

Day Two

1. Read John 8:31–32.

2. After reading this passage, do you think that Jesus would conclude that you are "really a disciple"? In other words, how do people see the light of Jesus in your life? What could people practically point to in your life that shows that you are shining the light of Jesus?

3. What do you think the relationship is between the importance of obedience and the reliance upon grace in your life? Which one do you emphasize more?

4. Real disciples follow Jesus obediently. Then what about those who have left the church and no longer follow Jesus? What can we say about them?

Day Three

1. Read John 8:34–38.

2. The world defines *freedom* as "do what I want to do." Jesus defines it very differently. Freedom means we are empowered to live with joy, peace, purpose, hope, love, kindness, selflessness, truthfulness, goodness, and everything that leads to fullness of life; while at the same time, we are free from all that kept us from life. Spend time reflecting and journaling on the freedom that Jesus has brought you.

3. If you have yet to work through past experiences that are hindering your relationship with God, what steps can you take today to start working through this pain and receive healing from Jesus? If you have worked through traumatic experiences, take the time to write about how the Lord has freed you and be encouraged by his work in your life.

4. If you are stuck and are not currently experiencing biblical freedom in your life, can you think of someone who could mentor and help you in the process?

Day Four

1. Read John 8:39–47.

2. In this passage, the Jewish people claim their heritage as children of Abraham. How often does our heritage, or our traditions, get in the way of true obedience to the words of Jesus?

3. This passage also talks about the devil. Do you think that the devil influences Christians today? In what way? Do you think that he has any influence in your life?

4. Walking in the light means that we can find our way because we can see clearly. We have a sense of direction and a sense of purpose. Jesus, the Light of the world, is our GPS. He guides us, and when we mess up, we hear "recalculating" so that we can get back on the right path. How does Jesus guide you back on the right path?

Day Five

1. Read John 8:12 one more time.

2. Pray through the entire passage verse by verse, allowing the deeper meaning that you have discovered lead you as you pray. Ask the Spirit to continue to remind you of what you have learned and to help you apply these truths to your life. Jot down any further applications that come to mind as you pray.

3. Turn back to the discussion questions from the video teaching (Discussion #1, #2). If there are questions that your group did not have time to discuss or questions that you might like to think more about, use this time to review and reflect further.

CALLED TO TESTIFY
Blind Man

◇

DR. LEON HARRIS

JOHN 9:1–18, 35–41

After saying this, he spit on the ground, made some mud with the saliva, and put it on the man's eyes. "Go," he told him, "wash in the Pool of Siloam" (this word means "Sent"). So the man went and washed, and came home seeing.

John 9:6–7

Pool of Siloam excavations
Location of Passage: Jerusalem

PART 1: DIGGING FOR MEANING

Jesus breaks two Jewish traditions, but he does so because he wants to heal a man from blindness.

Video Introduction by Bruce Marchiano
Video Scripture Reading: John 9:1–18, 35–41

◆ 3D magic eye pictures

◆ Physical vs. spiritual blindness

Blind man being led by a boy

◆ Sin as the cause of blindness

Consider now: Who, being innocent, has ever perished? Where were the upright ever destroyed? As I have observed, those who plow evil and those who sow trouble reap it. At the breath of God they perish; at the blast of his anger they are no more.

Job 4:7–9

◆ Jesus corrects their belief about suffering.

◆ Interpreting John 9:3

> *And we know that in all things God works for the good of those who love him.*
>
> Romans 8:28a

> *"We may translate it as follows: 'Neither this man nor his parents sinned,' said Jesus. 'But so that the work of God might be displayed in his life, we must do the work of him who sent me while it is still day.'"*
>
> —Gary Burge[45]

◆ Darkness vs. Light of the world

> *I, the LORD, have called you in righteousness; I will take hold of your hand. I will keep you and will make you to be a covenant for the people and a light for the Gentiles, to open eyes that are blind, to free captives from prison and to release from the dungeon those who sit in darkness.*
>
> Isaiah 42:6–7

◆ Jesus heals physical blindness.

◆ The testimony of the blind man.

He replied, "The man they call Jesus made some mud and put it on my eyes. He told me to go to Siloam and wash. So I went and washed, and then I could see." "Where is this man?" they asked him. "I don't know," he said.

John 9:11–12

◆ Pharisees vs. Jesus

Did You Know?

The making of the mud is a breach of the prohibition of kneading on the Sabbath. The placing of mud on the eyes would be included in the class of prohibited anointings. Healing on the Sabbath was forbidden unless the life was in danger.[47]

◆ The Pharisees question the blind man again.

"As the story progresses, Jesus is more closely revealed by name: He is 'Jesus' (9:10), then he is called a 'prophet' (9:17), then 'the Christ' (9:22), and finally, he is declared to be 'from God' (9:33)."

—Gary Burge[48]

He replied, "Whether he is a sinner or not, I don't know. One thing I do know. I was blind but now I see!"

John 9:25

Discussion #1

1. Jewish people of the first century thought that blindness was the result of sin. What would it be like to be blind or visually impaired in the first century and not be allowed to enter the synagogue, the market place, or get married?

2. The Jewish people of Jesus's day believed that the blind man was cursed by God for sin. Are there diseases or types of people that some today might judge as "cursed by God"? What could we do to make our churches more welcoming to them?

3. Do you believe that Jesus still brings people out of darkness into the light today? How have you experienced this in your own life?

4. Many people walk in darkness without realizing that they are not experiencing the abundant life that Jesus provides. Can you think of any characteristics that are common in Christians that you know (for example, greed or a critical spirit) that might hinder them from experiencing the abundant life?

PART 2: YOUR LIFE TODAY

Jesus is still the light of the world. How will you respond? Will you respond like the Pharisees or like the blind man?

◆ The seeing and the blind

> "Spiritual blindness or darkness is an even worse disease than physical blindness."
>
> —Leon Harris

◆ Curses for disobedience

> The LORD will afflict you with the boils of Egypt and with tumors, festering sores and the itch, from which you cannot be cured. The LORD will afflict you with madness, blindness and confusion of mind. At midday you will grope about like a blind person in the dark. You will be unsuccessful in everything you do; day after day you will be oppressed and robbed, with no one to rescue you.
>
> Deuteronomy 28:27–29

◆ The curses are reversed.

> *Then the man said, "Lord, I believe," and he worshiped him.*
>
> John 9:38

◆ The Pharisees

◆ How will you respond?

◆ One of the great promises God made to his people was that he would send a Savior to help those who are desperate—a promise that would be fulfilled by Jesus (Isaiah 42:6–7).

> *I am the light of the world. Whoever follows me will never walk in darkness, but will have the light of life.*
>
> John 8:12

◆ Will you respond by sharing your faith?

"Healing was important to Jesus' work, and likewise it should be important in the church's work today."

—Gary Burge[49]

◆ Tell your story.

◆ Our eyes are also opened to injustice and poverty.

◆ Bring the light of the gospel to the world.

Discussion #2

1. Explain which character you most identify with in John 9? The disciples who link sickness with sin? The neighbors who paid so little attention to the needy that they were not even sure that this was the blind man? The Pharisees who question and condemn? The blind man who worships Jesus?

2. Leon Harris urged us to "tell your story." Who have you told your story to? What was that experience like?

3. Think of one person who is spiritually blind. If the Lord allowed you to tell them your story and brought them to the light, how would their life change? How could you share your story with them this week?

4. Take some time to pray as you end the study, praying specifically for those with whom you can share your story this week.

PERSONAL REFLECTION

Day One

1. Read John 9:1–12.

2. Imagine that you are the blind man who has just been healed by Jesus. How would you feel? How would you respond?

3. You might not have been physically blind when Jesus found you, but you were certainly spiritually blind. In what ways has Jesus healed you, both physically and spiritually? Spend some time in prayer thanking him for the countless blessings in your life.

4. Begin to memorize the key verses for this passage: John 9:6–7.

Day Two

1. Read John 9:13–34.

2. Do you sometimes view all diseases and problems as the result of sin? When something bad happens to you, is your first response that you must have done something wrong and God is punishing you? What does John 9 teach you about this way of thinking?

3. The Pool of Siloam was probably a popular location for those seeking cleansing. Jesus sent the blind man there to complete his healing/cleansing. What kind of witness would this have been for those at the pool? Do you think that the blind man talked to people about Jesus after his healing? Do you tell others about God's healing in your life?

Day Three

1. Read John 9:35–41.

2. If you have never done so, take some time to write out your testimony, along with a basic outline of the gospel message. These two items will serve you well as you go forth to tell your story to this dark and blind world.

3. How has Jesus brought light into your life? What difference has this light made in your life? Spend some time thanking Jesus for this light.

Day Four

1. Read Matthew 20:29–34.

2. Do we in the church today have the compassion and love, like Jesus did, to see the needy and then to help them?

3. Consider those who are spiritually blind. What compassion/love and kinds of help do they need? Are there people in your life who are spiritually blind? Ask the Lord to give you a list of names.

4. God uses Christians to reach the world with his glorious good news. How are you allowing Jesus to work through you to reach this blind and dark world with the revelation that Jesus is the Light? Are there specific prayers or actions that you are taking to bring Jesus's light to them?

Day Five

1. Read John 9:1–18, 35–41 one more time.

2. Pray through the entire passage verse by verse, allowing the deeper meaning that you have discovered lead you as you pray. Ask the Spirit to continue to remind you of what you have learned and to help you apply these truths to your life. Jot down any further applications that come to mind as you pray.

3. Turn back to the discussion questions from the video teaching (Discussion #1, #2). If there are questions that your group did not have time to discuss or questions that you might like to think more about, use this time to review and reflect further.

CALLED TO SHEPHERD
Good Shepherd

DR. JEREMY TREAT

JOHN 10:1–16

*I am the good shepherd; I know my sheep and my sheep
know me—just as the Father knows me and I know the
Father—and I lay down my life for the sheep.*

John 10:14–15

Location of Passage: Jerusalem

PART 1: DIGGING FOR MEANING

A shepherd and sheep would spend so much time together out in the fields that the shepherd intimately knew the sheep—every single one.

Video Introduction by Bruce Marchiano
Video Scripture Reading: John 10:1–16

◆ Why did Jesus come?

> The thief comes only to steal and kill and destroy; I have come that they may have life, and have it to the full.
>
> John 10:10

◆ Life (*zoe*)

◆ How can we experience this life?

◆ We are sheep.

"This image [of being a sheep] should curb our rampant self-exaltation. On our best days we're still helpless sheep desperately in need of a shepherd."

—Matt Carter and Josh Wredberg[50]

We all, like sheep, have gone astray, each of us has turned to our own way; and the LORD has laid on him the iniquity of us all.

Isaiah 53:6

◆ Wolves and thieves

◆ False teachers

For the time will come when people will not put up with sound doctrine. Instead, to suit their own desires, they will gather around them a great number of teachers to say what their itching ears want to hear. They will turn their ears away from the truth and turn aside to myths.

2 Timothy 4:3–4

◆ The devil

◆ Jesus is the Good Shepherd.

> *His sheep follow him because they know his voice. . . .*
> *I am the good shepherd; I know my sheep and my sheep*
> *know me.*
>
> John 10:4b, 14

◆ The voice of the shepherd

> *"Jesus came and his sheep responded. Their response is*
> *simple: they hear, and they follow."*
>
> —Matt Carter and Josh Wredberg[51]

> *Simon Peter answered him, "Lord, to whom shall we go?*
> *You have the words of eternal life. We have come to believe*
> *and to know that you are the Holy One of God."*
>
> John 6:68–69

◆ Jesus lays down his life for his sheep.

> "[Jesus] cares for them so much, he is willing to come between his flock and danger, even to die for them . . . unwilling to sacrifice even one of his animals to satisfy the enemy."
>
> —Gary Burge[52]

◆ The cross

◆ Jesus won the battle.

> The reason my Father loves me is that I lay down my life—only to take it up again. No one takes it from me, but I lay it down of my own accord. I have authority to lay it down and authority to take it up again. This command I received from my Father.
>
> John 10:17–18

Discussion #1

1. Jeremy Treat said that the evil one comes not with tanks and bombs but with cunning questions, masked lies, and half-truths. What does that look like in your life? How does Satan try to trick you, or trick those in your church?

2. Jesus said that he "has come that they may have life." If someone were to follow you around for a week, would they be able to define what *life* is based on the way that you live? What are the main priorities of your life? What do you think you emphasize too much? Too little?

3. John 10 says that the sheep will recognize the voice of the shepherd. Do you think that God speaks to you? If so, how does he speak to you? Be specific.

4. Do we today recognize Jesus's voice? How can we recognize it from among the millions of voices/sounds that we hear today—amidst the noise of TV, cell phones, internet, etc.? How can we be sure that we are following Jesus and not some other voice, perhaps that of the thief or robber?

PART 2: YOUR LIFE TODAY

The Good Shepherd cares for us, but we are also called to care for others.

◆ The Good Shepherd cares for us.

Jesus as the Good Shepherd
Fresco, Vienna, 1911

Did You Know?

The Middle Eastern shepherd has a personal devotion to his sheep. He talks to them and sings to them. Often shepherds will carry a short flute and use a repeated tune so that the flock has a consistent auditory cue to follow.[53]

The LORD is my shepherd, I lack nothing. He makes me lie down in green pastures, he leads me beside quiet waters, he refreshes my soul. He guides me along the right paths for his name's sake. Even though I walk through the darkest valley, I will fear no evil, for you are with me; your rod and your staff, they comfort me. You prepare a table before me in the presence of my enemies. You anoint my head with oil; my cup overflows. Surely your goodness and love will follow me all the days of my life, and I will dwell in the house of the LORD forever.

Psalm 23

◆ Long for his presence (I lack nothing).

"Jesus doesn't promise us a trouble-free life. He promises us joy that is bigger and lasts longer than our troubles."

—Matt Carter and Josh Wredberg[54]

◆ Look for his direction (not the shadows).

◆ Listen to his voice (not the voice of others).

"Sheep who know the shepherd are not led astray."

—Robert Mounce[55]

◆ We are called to care for others.

I will place over them one shepherd, my servant David, and he will tend them; he will tend them and be their shepherd.

Ezekiel 34:23

◆ We are all *in* the flock, and we are called to care *for* the flock.

Discussion #2

1. Jesus is the good shepherd who leads us beside quiet waters. Do you normally think of Jesus as *good*? We can trust that he is good because he died on the cross for us. In what specific ways has he been good in your life?

2. Do you think that most Christians are willing to follow the Shepherd's leading, or is the idea of following what Jesus wants difficult for many? What about you?

3. Did anyone shepherd or mentor you when you were younger? How did that help you?

4. You are a shepherd in the service of King Jesus. We are both sheep and shepherd at the same time. We are Jesus's sheep, so he cares for and protects us; but we are also shepherds, so we care for and protect those Jesus has given us to care for. Do you see them? You don't have to be perfect to minister to others; you just have to be willing. How is your ministry of shepherding going?

PERSONAL REFLECTION

Day One

1. Read John 10.

2. John 10, along with Psalm 23, show us that the Shepherd wants to guide us. He leads and guides us along right paths for his name's sake. In fact, he will guide us to "green pastures." In what area are you seeking the Shepherd's guidance today?

3. In the first century, the term *shepherd* also contained the idea of authority. Are you submitting to Jesus's authority in your life? Ask Jesus if there are areas that you still need to submit to him.

4. His power/authority also means that he can protect the sheep. First Peter 5:8 reminds us that we need a protector with authority because "your enemy the devil prowls around like a roaring lion looking for someone to devour." Thank your Shepherd for protecting you today and ask him to protect you in any area that comes to mind: family, friends, job, etc.

5. Begin to memorize the key verses for this passage: John 10:14–15.

Day Two

1. Read Ezekiel 34, thinking about John 10 as you read it.

2. Take some time and allow the truth of John 10 and Ezekiel 34 to fully sink in. Listen to Ezekiel 34 (audio available at www.biblegateway.com). Let the Lord rescue you afresh from any current problems in your life. Ask the Good Shepherd to help you to see how he sees you. Write down how that prayer time went.

3. Just as the Good Shepherd rescued you, he also wants to rescue others in the world who are still in darkness—and he often uses us in this rescue project. What people are you a shepherd over? Is your shepherding going well or not so well?

4. Sheep need to be led to water each day, protected each day, cared for each day, and given food each day. If the shepherd does not do this each day, the sheep will die. We as shepherds need to be patient and have compassion with those who are in our care, every single day. Is this difficult for you to do? Ask the Lord to increase your patience for those you care for.

Day Three

1. Read Psalm 23.

2. Sheep follow their shepherd because they know his voice. Do you know Jesus's voice?

3. What does God's voice sound like when he speaks to you? In the Old Testament, for Samuel, it sounded like Eli (1 Samuel 3:1–10). For others, it might be a feeling, an image, or God might speak through the Bible or through a friend, or in dreams, or even in our thoughts. Your task is to discern whose voice is speaking: is it God, you, the thief, culture? How can you better discern God's voice from competing voices? Any ideas? Spend some time in prayer about this idea, asking the Lord for discernment.

Day Four

1. Read 1 Peter 5:1–3 and Colossians 2:13–15.

2. In John 10:10, the thief is trying to steal, kill, and destroy. Thankfully, the Good Shepherd is more powerful. Meditate on and thank God for the truth of Colossians 2:13–15.

3. First Peter 5:8 and Revelation 12:12 tell us that the battle continues today. Just as Jesus fought on the cross over two thousand years ago on our behalf, he still fights on our behalf today. He also empowers us to join in the battle with his authority. Have you joined in the battle, or are you sitting on the sidelines?

4. False shepherds abound in our day, promising all kinds of false securities. Flee from them. Seek safety and guidance only from the Good Shepherd. All others are fake copies and will leave you empty handed—or worse. How has the enemy tried to trick you with a fake copy?

Day Five

1. Read John 10 one more time.

2. Pray through the entire passage verse by verse, allowing the deeper meaning that you have discovered lead you as you pray. Ask the Spirit to continue to remind you of what you have learned and to help you apply these truths to your life. Jot down any further applications that come to mind as you pray.

3. Turn back to the discussion questions from the video teaching (Discussion #1, #2). If there are questions that your group did not have time to discuss or questions that you might like to think more about, use this time to review and reflect further.

CALLED TO BE A LIVING WITNESS
Lazarus

◇

DR. SEAN McDOWELL

JOHN 11:1–7, 17–27, 34–44

When he had said this, Jesus called in a loud voice, "Lazarus, come out!" The dead man came out, his hands and feet wrapped with strips of linen, and a cloth around his face.

John 11:43–44a

Location of Passage: Bethany

PART 1: DIGGING FOR MEANING

What do you do when Jesus doesn't show up to take care of your problems? Mary and Martha experienced the devastating death of their brother, Lazarus, and Jesus was nowhere to be found.

Video Introduction by Bruce Marchiano
Video Scripture Reading: John 11:1–7, 17–27, 34–44

◆ Doubt when Jesus doesn't show up

◆ Jesus's four-day delay is very troubling:

  ◇ Shame-honor culture

> ### Did You Know?
>
> Friends were expected to drop everything and go immediately when summoned, and had the "right" to immediate assistance.[56]

  ◇ Financial struggle

  ◇ The Good Shepherd

146

I am the good shepherd. The good shepherd lays down his life for the sheep.

John 10:11

◆ Jesus waited two days before going to Lazarus.

◆ Why did Jesus wait two days?

Did You Know?

Jews would return to a cemetery after three days to check to see if the person was living.[57] One Jewish text says, "For three days the soul returns to the grave, thinking that it will return [into the body]; when however, it sees that the color of its face has changed, then it goes away and leaves it."[58]

◆ After three days, it was too late.

"Lord," Martha said to Jesus, "if you had been here, my brother would not have died. But I know that even now God will give you whatever you ask."

John 11:21–22

◆ Is Martha expecting Jesus to raise her brother from the dead?

◆ At the grave, Martha has no hope.

◆ Yet, Martha *still* believes in Jesus.

"Yes, Lord," she replied, "I believe that you are the Messiah, the Son of God, who is to come into the world."

John 11:27

◆ Faith despite . . .

◆ Lazarus was four days dead.

bad odor
& after 3-4 days they
can't come alive, or
so the Jews thought —

Tomb of Lazarus in Bethany

"In raising Lazarus, Jesus is rescuing Martha and Mary as well."

—Bruce Malina and Richard Rohrbaugh[59]

◆ Responses to Jesus's miracle: an apologetics angle

3 days soul return
to grave
No chance of life
after 3 days —
impossible for
Jesus to raise
Lazarus from
the dead.

Why did Jesus wait
2 days - Different type
of miracle.

"Most of those present recognized Jesus' power, but even some of the witnesses became Jesus' betrayers."

—Craig Keener[60]

◆ Religious leaders

Therefore, many of the Jews who had come to visit Mary, and had seen what Jesus did, believed in him. But some of them went to the Pharisees and told them what Jesus had done. . . . So from that day on they plotted to take his life.

John 11:45–46, 53

◆ Miracles do not always lead to faith.

◆ Mary and Martha

didn't thin Lazarus was going to come
Out a live.
But they both still believed in Jesus.
Faith to spite disappointment

◆ Faith even when we do not see

Now faith is confidence in what we hope for and assurance about what we do not see.

Hebrews 11:1

◆ Examples of faith in Hebrews 11

◆ Faith is trusting despite disappointment . . .

◆ . . . but this does not mean that faith is blind.

Discussion #1

1. Jesus raised Lazarus from the dead on the fourth day, which was "impossible." Is any situation that you might be in today "impossible" for Jesus?

2. When you first read John 11:21–22, did you think that Martha expected Jesus to immediately raise her brother from the dead? Sean McDowell taught that Martha was not expecting Jesus to raise her brother from the dead. What do you think she was saying to Jesus in these verses?

3. Jesus *teaches* in John 11:25, "I am the resurrection and the life." Although Martha has faith in Jesus's words, it is when Jesus *does* the miracle of resurrecting Lazarus to life that she can fully understand Jesus's teaching. What is the relationship between our teaching and our actions, specifically miracles? Do you think our ministries today should only be teaching/preaching, or should they include miraculous actions?

4. The examples of faith in Hebrews 11 show that believers in God do not always have a good or "successful" life. Do you think that most Christians today feel like they deserve a "good life" if they are followers of Jesus? How would you define a good life?

PART 2: YOUR LIFE TODAY

Keep believing in Jesus, even when he does not show up the way that you want. Easy to say—much more difficult to live.

◆ How often are we "disappointed" by Jesus?

◆ Mary and Martha believed before . . .

Tomb of Lazarus in Bethany

◆ Jesus meets people in the midst of their difficulties: "Lord, if you had been here . . . "

"Mary (like her sister) . . . is overcome with grief (11:33). The NIV's "weeping" leaves the impression of quiet tears of sadness, but the Greek . . . describes loud wailing and crying."

—Gary Burge[61]

"Remember that Jesus also experienced grief along with Martha and Mary in the passage, as he was 'deeply moved in spirit and troubled' (11:33) and 'Jesus wept' (11:35)."

—Matt Williams

◆ Nabeel Qureshi

> *Who shall separate us from the love of Christ? Shall trouble or hardship or persecution or famine or nakedness or danger or sword? As it is written: "For your sake we face death all day long; we are considered as sheep to be slaughtered." No, in all these things we are more than conquerors through him who loved us. For I am convinced that neither death nor life, neither angels nor demons, neither the present nor the future, nor any powers, neither height nor depth, nor anything else in all creation, will be able to separate us from the love of God that is in Christ Jesus our Lord.*
>
> Romans 8:35–39

◆ Inaugurated kingdom

> *Three times I pleaded with the Lord to take it away from me. But he said to me, "My grace is sufficient for you, for my power is made perfect in weakness."*
>
> 2 Corinthians 12:8–9a

◆ Jesus understands suffering.

Therefore, since we have a great high priest who has ascended into heaven, Jesus the Son of God, let us hold firmly to the faith we profess. For we do not have a high priest who is unable to empathize with our weaknesses, but we have one who has been tempted in every way, just as we are—yet he did not sin. Let us then approach God's throne of grace with confidence, so that we may receive mercy and find grace to help us in our time of need.

Hebrews 4:14–16

◆ Is it okay to struggle in our faith?

◆ But what happens when God doesn't do anything?

"Death has been swallowed up in victory." "Where, O death, is your victory? Where, O death, is your sting?" The sting of death is sin, and the power of sin is the law. But thanks be to God! He gives us the victory through our Lord Jesus Christ.

1 Corinthians 15:54–57

"Death will not gain the final word in [Lazarus's] life. The tragedy is not by God's design, but God will use it, making it an opportunity to glorify his Son."

—Gary Burge[62]

◆ We are called to life and faith so that we can be living witnesses of Jesus's life to all around us.

◆ Life to the spiritually dead

> *"The message of resurrection is that the relationship with Jesus that begins now, in faith, has a future through the believer's own resurrection."*
>
> —Craig Koester[63]

◆ Our identity: raised to life

◆ Our purpose: witness to this life, even in difficult circumstances

Discussion #2

1. What impossible (or difficult) situation are you facing today?

2. Have you found a kind of "faith despite disappointment" in your own life? How are you trusting in God even when he does not show up in the way that you think he should?

3. Sean McDowell talked about *inaugurated eschatology*, that the kingdom of God is here, but not fully here. As a result, we do not always see God act the way that we would want him to act. Do you believe that God's plans are bigger than ours, and that he can be trusted even when we don't understand? Is it difficult or easy to believe this?

4. Sometimes it helps to remember God's past faithfulness to trust him in the present storms. How has God been faithful to you in your past? How have you seen him be faithful to others in their lives?

5. Take some time to give thanks to God in prayer.

PERSONAL REFLECTION

Day One

1. Read John 11:1–27.

2. Are there areas in your life where you feel (or have felt in the past) that Jesus didn't show up or that he disappointed you? How did his absence make you feel?

3. Spend some time thinking about—and perhaps journaling about—how you can have the same type of faith as Martha. She trusted in Jesus, despite feeling abandoned by Jesus and by God. Do you have any ideas on how you can continue to trust Jesus in your difficulty?

4. Begin to memorize the key verses for this passage: John 11:43–44a.

Day Two

1. Read John 11:34–44.

2. What difference does it make in your life today that Jesus has power over the tomb?

3. How can learning about John 11 affect your thoughts/feelings when you attend funerals?

4. What or whom should we fear given that Jesus is with us, the good, powerful Shepherd?

Day Three

1. Read Mark 5:21–24, 35–43.

2. Lazarus does not say a word in John 11. Using your imagination, what do you think he would have said if we could hear him talk?

3. With whom do you relate to the most in John 11? Lazarus, Martha, Mary, Jesus, the Jewish leaders? Why?

Day Four

1. Read John 20:1–9.

2. What was the potential cost of Jesus going to Bethany to minister to Lazarus (see John 10:31; 11:8)? What does that say about our own ministries, and the potential cost we might pay to minister to others? Can you list some examples of times when you have "paid a price" to minister to others?

3. When Jesus rescues Lazarus, he also rescues his sisters, Mary and Martha, who now have their male support system restored to them. Remember that when you minister to people, you are not just helping them, but all the people that they will touch in their lives. Spend some time considering the people that you have ministered to, and think about the full extent of the reach of that ministry.

4. Since God does the impossible, like raising Lazarus on the fourth day, don't be afraid to pray *big* prayers to a *big* God. Take some time to pray some big prayers right now: for yourself, family, friends, neighborhood, church, your town, missionaries you know, the unreached people in the world, those who will suffer for the name of Jesus today.

Day Five

1. Read John 11:1–27, 34–44 one more time.

2. Pray through the entire passage verse by verse, allowing the deeper meaning that you have discovered lead you as you pray. Ask the Spirit to continue to remind you of what you have learned and to help you apply these truths to your life. Jot down any further applications that come to mind as you pray.

3. Turn back to the discussion questions from the video teaching (Discussion #1, #2). If there are questions that your group did not have time to discuss or questions that you might like to think more about, use this time to review and reflect further.

CALLED TO SERVE IN LOVE
Last Supper

◇

DR. MARK STRAUSS

JOHN 13:1–17

After that, he poured water into a basin and began to wash his disciples' feet, drying them with the towel that was wrapped around him.

John 13:5

Interior of traditional Upper Room
Location of Passage: The upper room, Jerusalem.

PART 1: DIGGING FOR MEANING

At the Last Supper, Jesus shocks his disciples by washing their feet. In that culture, only a slave washed someone's feet since it was degrading and humiliating to do so.

It is impressive when someone with position and power relinquishes that for the good of others.

Video Introduction by Bruce Marchiano
Video Scripture Reading: John 13:1–17

◆ King George VI and Queen Elizabeth during World War II

◆ The King of kings was willing to give up his position of power and glory to come to earth and serve us.

◆ Three things that are drawing near:

◇ 1. The Passover is drawing near.

Passover Seder plate with matzah and wine

◇ The significance of Passover in Israel's history

Did You Know?

In the Passover meal, a portion of the unleavened bread was broken off with the understanding that the Messiah would eat it when he comes and celebrates with Israel. Jesus distributed this portion to his disciples and declared, "This is my body." Jesus identified himself as the Messiah.[64]

◇ Jesus is the Passover Lamb.

The next day John saw Jesus coming toward him and said, "Look, the Lamb of God, who takes away the sin of the world!"

John 1:29

◇ 2. Jesus's departure is drawing near.

"Jesus knew that the hour had come for him to leave this world and go to the Father."

John 13:1b

◇ The *hour*

◇ Code words *points to Salvation*

Glorify

◇ Jesus's departure is not abandonment.

to accomplish their salvation
"It is finish" Our sins have
been paid for -

> Having loved his own, he loved them to the end.
>
> John 13:1c

◇ 3. Judas's betrayal is drawing near.

John 13: 2

> In different ways, all the disciples betray Jesus, not just Judas.[65]

◆ Jesus washes the disciples' feet.

John 13: 4-5

◆ Cultural context of foot washing

◆ Foot washing is a symbol of loving devotion and sacrificial service.

[handwritten: Jesus is the ~~enlightenment~~ Enlightenment act.]

Did You Know?

Foot washing was a task performed by gentile slaves or sometimes by wives or children, never by a superior on an inferior, never by a rabbi on his disciples.[67]

◆ Foot washing is a symbol of the washing away of our sins through Jesus's death.

◆ Peter and Jesus's conversation

He came to Simon Peter, who said to him, "Lord, are you going to wash my feet?" Jesus replied, "You do not realize now what I am doing, but later you will understand."

John 13:6–7

◆ Peter doesn't understand.

He struggles to wash their feet. Peter is shocked that Jesus is doing this.

Jesus Washing Peter's Feet
by Ford Madox Brown

◆ Peter overreacts.

John 13: 9

"Then, Lord," Simon Peter replied, "not just my feet but my hands and my head as well!"

John 13:9

◆ What does it mean to "wash your feet"?

One bath - "Our salvation"
Titus 3: 4-5   John 13: 16
1 John 1: 9   2 Corin 8: 9
John 13: 12-13

If we confess our sins, he is faithful and just and will forgive us our sins and purify us from all unrighteousness.

1 John 1:9

◆ Significance of foot washing

◇ 1. Jesus does not relinquish his authority.

Foot washing scene on ivory diptych,
14th century, France

Very truly I tell you, no servant is greater than his master, nor is a messenger greater than the one who sent him.

John 13:16

◇ 2. Jesus uses his power for the benefit of others.

For you know the grace of our Lord Jesus Christ, that though he was rich, yet for your sake he became poor, so that you through his poverty might become rich.

2 Corinthians 8:9

"This was a model of unbelievable love, to wash the feet of the very one who would send him to his death!"

—Grant Osborne[69]

Discussion #1

1. What would you do if you received "all power," as Jesus did in John 13:3? Do you think that you would sacrificially serve others, or would you have other plans?

   There would be Peace —
   Would you be vendictive of your enemies
   if you had all power.

2. How does it make you feel to know that the Savior of the world willingly did a slave's job to sacrificially serve by washing feet?

3. Learning about the cultural context of foot washing in the first century brings a new depth to this passage. In a shame-honor culture, Jesus the master washed the disciples' feet—their dirty, stinking, excrement covered feet. What do you think and how do you feel when you learn that feet in the first century were covered with human and animal excrement?

4. Why do you think Peter did not want Jesus to wash his feet? If Jesus walked up to you today and offered to wash your feet, would you let him? Why or why not? What would it mean to you to have Jesus wash your feet?

PART 2: YOUR LIFE TODAY

Christ's sacrificial service brings us salvation and is a model for our own service to others.

◆ Jesus washed the disciples' feet to illustrate two things:

◇ First, Jesus came to serve.

He accomplished our salvation.

> The Son of Man came not to be served, but to serve, and to give his life as a ransom for many.
>
> Mark 10:45

◇ Second, Jesus came to purify us.

Symbolize washing away our sins

◆ Three applications:

◇ 1. Christ's sacrificial service is the means of our salvation.

It is holy a gift from God.

Philippians 2

◇ Why did Jesus need to become a human?

Human being had sinned, so they had to pay the price

Hebrew 2:14, 17

169

> *Since the children have flesh and blood, he too shared in their humanity so that by his death he might break the power of him who holds the power of death. . . . For this reason he had to be made like them, fully human in every way, in order that he might become a merciful and faithful high priest in service to God, and that he might make atonement for the sins of the people.*
>
> Hebrews 2:14, 17

◇ Why couldn't we pay the price?

We were dead spiritually.
Since Adam + Eve.

> *As for you, you were dead in your transgressions and sins, in which you used to live when you followed the ways of this world and of the ruler of the kingdom of the air. . . . But because of his great love for us, God, who is rich in mercy, made us alive with Christ even when we were dead in transgressions—it is by grace you have been saved.*
>
> Ephesians 2:1–5

◇ 2. Service is the model or example for us: we are called to serve in love.

> "The authority by which the Christian leader leads is not power but love, not force but example, not coercion but reasoned persuasion. Leaders have power, but power is safe only in the hands of those who humble themselves to serve."
>
> —John Stott[70]

"To follow Jesus by humbly serving our brothers and sisters requires a fundamental transformation of our nature. We are selfish, independent, arrogant sinners with cold, hard hearts—what Jesus demands from us is to live as selfless, trusting, humble servants."

—Matt Carter and Josh Wredberg[71]

◇ 3. Service is the key to reaching the world for Christ.

Serve others as God served us —

◇ Conventional first-century wisdom

◆ Jesus's radical new ethic

Ephesians 4: 11-12

"[Jesus] assumes his battle dress [in the conflict with evil] by laying down his garments, girding himself with a towel, and taking up a basin to wash feet."

—Craig Koester[72]

Love your enemies, do good to those who hate you, bless those who curse you, pray for those who mistreat you.

Luke 6:27–28

Discussion #2

1. According to Mark Strauss, Jesus's radical new ethic is one of love. Instead of fighting for one's rights, do you think that humbling oneself to sacrificially serve others in love can lead to positive results? Do you think it was wise for the church to serve donuts to the atheists, as Strauss explained, or should they have fought for their right to worship at the foot of the cross on Easter on that hillside in Southern California?

2. Jesus tells the disciples that they are "clean" (John 13:10). Really? These disciples who have blown it so often are clean? If Jesus walked up to you today, would he declare that you are clean? Is it hard to believe that you are clean?

3. What might be today's equivalents to the work of foot washing?

4. Can you think of any sacrificial service that you or others have done that are examples of foot washing? What are you giving up today to serve others so that they can find wholeness in the Lord? There is a world of hurt out there that needs our help. They are oppressed, like sheep without a shepherd. You can make a difference as you serve!

5. Take some time to pray as you end the study.

PERSONAL REFLECTION

Day One

1. Read John 13:1–17.

2. If you were present at the Last Supper, how shocked would you have been when Jesus the Master began to wash feet? Do you think that Jesus would have washed your feet? Why or why not? Would it have been difficult to allow him to wash your feet?

3. Prayerfully reflect further on the statement "you are clean." Do you feel clean? Why or why not? If yes, take some time to thank Jesus for his forgiveness. If not, take some time to pray for forgiveness and for acceptance of the belief that those who confess their sins are forgiven (see Psalm 51:7; Isaiah 1:18; John 1:29; Romans 13:14). Clothe yourself with Christ and his purity. Ask the Lord to forgive you anew and declare afresh: "You are clean!"

4. Begin to memorize the key verse for this passage: John 13:5.

Day Two

1. Read John 13:18–27.

2. Focus today on Mark Strauss's application, "Christ's sacrificial service is the means of our salvation." Are you ever tempted to think that you can atone for your own sins through doing good works? Is that even possible? Spend some time in prayer asking for forgiveness and thanking God for his forgiveness (read 1 John 1:9).

3. Do you think it was easy or hard for Jesus to become a human and experience all of humanity's temptations? What does God's willingness to become a human show us about the depth of his love for us and his desire that we find salvation?

Day Three

1. Read Luke 22:7–34.

2. Focus today on Mark Strauss's application, "Service is the model or example for us." Peter told Jesus, "You shall never wash my feet." Do you struggle with allowing Jesus to serve you? Do you feel that you have to be "good enough" to allow him to serve you? Are you willing to allow Jesus to forgive you? To cleanse you? To remove your shame? To empower you to serve others? Have you learned that it is only through Jesus that we can do anything (John 15:5)?

3. In a sense, serving others is death to our self and our own desires, which is difficult. Do you find it easy or hard to serve others?

4. Reflect right now on someone that you could lovingly serve today, and then remember Jesus's words: "Now that you know these things, you will be blessed if you do them" (John 13:17).

Day Four

1. Read Matthew 26:17–35.

2. Focus today on Mark Strauss's application, "Service is the key to reaching the world for Christ." Jesus exemplified servant love and sacrificial love. Typical first-century wisdom was to love your friends, but hate your enemies. Do you think most people today think the same? What about those in the church?

3. First John 3:18 instructs Christians to love others "in truth." What do you think loving others in truth means? What happens when we emphasize one over the other too much—love without truth, or truth without love? How can you keep those two in balance in your life? Think of specific people and specific ways that you could love them in truth this week.

4. When you think of reaching the world with the love of Jesus, do you think more of sharing words of the gospel message, or of acts of kindness? Jesus did both—he preached the gospel with both words and with actions. As we love others today, may we also share the truth of the gospel message in words, and not by actions alone.

Day Five

1. Read John 13 one more time.

2. Pray through the entire passage verse by verse, allowing the deeper meaning that you have discovered lead you as you pray. Ask the Spirit to continue to remind you of what you have learned and to help you apply these truths to your life. Jot down any further applications that come to mind as you pray.

3. Turn back to the discussion questions from the video teaching (Discussion #1, #2). If there are questions that your group did not have time to discuss or questions that you might like to think more about, use this time to review and reflect further. Pray a thanksgiving prayer that Jesus loves you and served you by providing for your salvation, and then pray that his model will be reproduced as you lovingly and sacrificially serve others in your own life.

CALLED TO BEAR FRUIT
I Am the True Vine

◇

DR. JOANNE JUNG

JOHN 15:1–17

*I am the vine; you are the branches. If you remain in me
and I in you, you will bear much fruit; apart from me
you can do nothing.*

John 15:5

Interior of traditional Upper Room
Location of Passage: Jerusalem, perhaps still in the Upper Room,
or perhaps near the temple, in sight of the vine that hung on the temple

PART 1: DIGGING FOR MEANING

God is described as the gardener. His intent is to produce fruit through the relationship between Jesus, the vine, and us, the branches.

Video Introduction by Bruce Marchiano
Video Scripture Reading: John 15:1–17

◆ Jesus is leaving.

How to stay connected w/ Jesus
Jesus is the vein + we are the branches.

◆ Pruning

> *"Fruitlessness not only threatens fire, but robs God of the glory rightly his."*
>
> —D. A. Carson[73]

◆ Israel as the vine

Did You Know?

Above the curtain at the entrance to the Holy Place in the temple was a gigantic grapevine of pure gold, representing Israel. Josephus claims that some of the grape clusters were the 'height of a man.'[74]

◆ Israel did not produce good fruit.

> *The vineyard of the LORD Almighty is the nation of Israel, and the people of Judah are the vines he delighted in. And he looked for justice, but saw bloodshed; for righteousness, but heard cries of distress.*
>
> Isaiah 5:7

& perfect.

◆ Jesus is the true vine.

He superseeds the vine of Israel

> *Remain in me, as I also remain in you. No branch can bear fruit by itself; it must remain in the vine. Neither can you bear fruit unless you remain in me.*
>
> John 15:4

◆ Remain in Jesus.

Stay tight with Jesus -

◆ Home

◆ Four characteristics of fruit:

◇ 1. Love for one another

Jesus is the true + perfect vine —
Jesus laid down his love for his friends —

> **Did You Know?**
>
> The apostle Paul told the Corinthian believers that no matter what ministry they exercised, if it was not carried out with love it counted for nothing in God's sight (1 Cor. 13:1–3).[75]

A new command I give you: Love one another. As I have loved you, so you must love one another. By this everyone will know that you are my disciples, if you love one another.

John 13:34–35

◇ 2. Evangelism and missions

Pruning is painful but sometime useful.

"Fruitfulness . . . includes both the production of Christian character and the winning of others to follow Christ."

—Leon Morris[76]

But these are written that you may believe that Jesus is the Messiah, the Son of God, and that by believing you may have life in his name.

John 20:31

◇ 3. Pray in his name.

Father, if you are willing, take this cup from me; yet not my will, but yours be done.

Luke 22:42

◇ 4. Joy

 John Verse 11

I have told you this so that my joy may be in you and that your joy may be complete.

John 15:11

Happiness vs. joy

Jesus is leaving . . .

Discussion #1

1. Joanne Jung said that pruning is necessary, but is sometimes painful. Can you recall examples from your life where God was pruning you? How did it feel? How did it turn out? Was it worth it?

2. Joanne Jung mentioned four "fruits" that come as a result of remaining in Jesus. Do you see those fruits in your local church? Do you see them in your life? Can you give examples of each?

3. Do you think it is true that apart from Jesus we can do nothing? Do you live as if that were true? What would change if you started to live really believing that this is true?

4. How can the disciples find joy when their Messiah is leaving? They left everything to follow Jesus—family, homes, jobs, future— and now Jesus is leaving. What have you left to follow Jesus? What emotions did you feel during that time?

through prayer - test your faith

PART 2: YOUR LIFE TODAY

Failure to stay close to Jesus leads to a lack of love, evangelistic fruit, and answered prayers.

◆ Abide

*I in you + you in me –
mummy – I'm little + God is Big
so you must see Jesus through
me!! :)*

◆ How do we foster abiding?

> "[Christianity] is a way of believing (doctrine) and a way of living (ethics), but these are nurtured by the life-giving connection with Jesus Christ."
>
> —Gary Burge[77]

◆ Get into his Word.

◆ Get his Word into us.

> *"Remaining in love is not automatic and will require . . . obedience to Jesus' words."*
>
> —Andrew Lincoln[78]

◆ Loving others

◆ Joy

Discussion #2

1. Jesus says that we must *remain* in him. (Other Bible translations say, *abide, dwell, stay joined, remain united, remain joined, live in, stay tight with*.) What do you think it means in our daily lives to remain in Jesus? Can you give specific examples of actions or attitudes in your life that help you to remain in Jesus?

   What would please Jesus.
   Living the life that would please Jesus
   Thankful, Grateful. Sunsets + Sunrise

2. Joanne Jung talked about getting into the Word of God, and allowing the Word of God to get into us, emphasizing both the mind and the heart aspects of the Christian life. How important are these two spiritual disciplines to you? What difference does knowing the contents of the Bible make in our lives?

   Uniting, fellowship ~

3. How do you incorporate daily spiritual practices like Bible reading, meditation, and memorization into your life? If you don't currently practice any spiritual disciplines, allow this time of sharing to encourage you and give you ideas on how you might start.

4. Loving God and loving people are one result of remaining in Jesus. Would someone who watched your life for a week agree that *love* characterizes your life?

5. Take some time to pray as you end the study.

PERSONAL REFLECTION

Day One

1. Read John 15:1–17.

2. Some fruits that we will bear when we remain in Jesus are evangelism and missions. Are these fruits found in your life? If not, how could you increase their importance?

3. Praying "in his name" means that we pray according to Jesus's will. How can you know what God's will is in your life? How can you pray when you don't know his will?

4. Begin to memorize the key verse for this passage: John 15:5.

Day Two

1. Read Galatians 5:13–26.

2. Do you agree with Joanne Jung that a key element of remaining in Jesus is allowing his word to dwell in your life? What spiritual disciplines do you practice that include the Bible? If Bible reading is not a major part of your life, are you ready to start a reading program? (Phone apps are a great way to start!)

3. How important is it to you to remain in Jesus? Do you think about Jesus during your day? Are you intimately connected to him? Have you laid before him everyone and everything that might hinder your relationship with him? Have you laid your fears about the future before him? Take some time in prayer to do these things.

Day Three

1. Read Matthew 7:15–29.

2. Joanne Jung shared a story about her mother-in-law. Are there people in your life that are more difficult to love? Do any names come to mind? What would the Lord want you to do to increase your love toward these people?

3. The term *prunes* in John 15:2 literally means "cleanses." God's response to sin is cleansing/pruning. Do you allow him to cleanse you when you stray from the vine? Ask the Lord to search your heart for sin, and then ask for forgiveness.

Day Four

1. Read Colossians 3:1–17.

2. To remain in Jesus means that we live our entire lives within the sphere of Jesus. His life and teachings influence and affect *everything* that we say, think, and do. Is this your experience of Jesus, or does he play a smaller role in your life? Are there things in your life that you are tempted to look to for life instead of Jesus?

3. Do you trust Jesus and Jesus *alone* to be your future and hope? Have you realized yet that remaining in Jesus is the only way to bear true and lasting fruit? If you do, you will find that those who trust in the Lord will not only rise up on eagle's wings (Isaiah 40:29–31), but will become joyful fruit bearers for the Lord! Ask the Lord to strengthen you and increase your joy.

Day Five

1. Read John 15:1–17 one more time.

2. Pray through the entire passage verse by verse, allowing the deeper meaning that you have discovered lead you as you pray. Ask the Spirit to continue to remind you of what you have learned and to help you apply these truths to your life. Jot down any further applications that come to mind as you pray.

3. Turn back to the discussion questions from the video teaching (Discussion #1, #2). If there are questions that your group did not have time to discuss or questions that you might like to think more about, use this time to review and reflect further.

NOTES

1. George R. Beasley-Murray, *John*, Word Biblical Commentaries, vol. 36. 2nd ed. (Nashville: Thomas Nelson, 1995), 35.
2. Andrew T. Lincoln, *The Gospel According to Saint John*, Black's New Testament Commentary (Peabody, Mass.: Hendrickson, 2005), 127.
3. Craig R. Koester, *The Word of Life: A Theology of John's Gospel* (Grand Rapids: Eerdmans, 2008), 187.
4. Craig S. Keener, *The Gospel of John: A Commentary*. 2 vols. (Peabody, Mass.: Hendrickson, 2003), 329.
5. Robert H. Mounce, *John*. The Expositor's Bible Commentary. Rev. ed. (Grand Rapids: Zondervan, 2007), 390.
6. Leon Morris, *Reflections on the Gospel of John* (Peabody, Mass.: Hendrickson, 2000), 80.
7. Matt Carter and Josh Wredberg, *Exalting Jesus in John*, Christ-Centered Exposition (Nashville: B&H, 2017), 51.
8. Craig R. Koester, *Symbolism in the Fourth Gospel* (Minneapolis: Fortress Press, 2003), 88–89.
9. Gary M. Burge, *John*, The NIV Application Commentary (Grand Rapids: Zondervan, 2000), 101.
10. Leon Morris, *The Gospel According to John*, New International Commentary on the New Testament (Grand Rapids: Eerdmans, 1995), 186.
11. Richard Bauckham, *Jesus and the Eyewitnesses: The Gospels as Eyewitness Testimony*. 2nd ed. (Grand Rapids: Eerdmans, 2017), 170
12. Keener, *John*, 539.
13. Keener, *John*, 544.
14. Morris, *Gospel According to John*, 201.
15. Gary M. Burge, *Encounters with Jesus* (Grand Rapids: Zondervan, 2010), 118.
16. Keener, *John*, 567.
17. Donald A. Carson, *The Gospel According to John*, The Pillar New Testament Commentary (Grand Rapids: Eerdmans, 1991), 216.
18. Mishnah, Niddah 4:1
19. Pirkei Abot 1:5.
20. Carson, *John*, 221.
21. Burge, *Encounters*, 102.
22. Morris, *Gospel According to John*, 230.
23. Burge, *Encounters*, 107.
24. Keener, *John*, 617.
25. Burge, *Encounters*, 108.
26. Lincoln, *John*, 182.
27. Gary M. Burge, *Gospel of John*, Bible Knowledge Background Commentary: John's Gospel, Hebrews-Revelation, ed. Craig A. Evans, (Colorado Springs: Cook Communications, 2005), 65
28. J. Randall Price and H. Wayne House, *Zondervan Handbook of Biblical Archaeology* (Grand Rapids: Zondervan, 2017).
29. Morris, *Gospel According to John*, 268.
30. http://www.thenazareneway.com/sabbath/39_prohib_sabbath.htm
31. Carson, *John*, 247.
32. Carter and Wredberg, *Exalting*, 124.

33. Beasley-Murray, *John*, 106.
34. Burge, *John*, Bible Knowledge, 85.
35. Colin G. Kruse, *John*, Tyndale New Testament Commentaries (Grand Rapids: Eerdmans, 2003), 193.
36. Morris, *Gospel According to John*, 348.
37. Koester, *The Word of Life*, 209.
38. Morris, *Gospel According to John*, 378.
39. Carson, *John*, 337.
40. Carson, *John*, 337.
41. Keener, *John*, 761.
42. J. Ramsey Michaels, *The Gospel According to John*, New International Commentary on the New Testament (Grand Rapids: Eerdmans, 2010), 491–492.
43. Keener, *John*, 740.
44. Burge, *John*, NIV Application, 256.
45. Burge, *John*, NIV Application, 272–273.
46. Talmud, Tractate Shabbath, Folio 108.
47. Morris, *Gospel According to John*, 427.
48. Burge, *John*, NIV Application, 275.
49. Burge, *John*, NIV Application, 280.
50. Carter and Wredberg, *Exalting*, 216.
51. Carter and Wredberg, *Exalting*, 215.
52. Burge, *John*, Bible Knowledge, 99.
53. Burge, *John*, Bible Knowledge, 98.
54. Carter and Wredberg, *Exalting*, 217.
55. Mounce, *John*, 501.
56. Bruce J. Malina and Richard L. Rohrbaugh, *Social-Science Commentary on the Gospel of John* (Minneapolis: Fortress Press, 1998), 195.
57. Talmud Tractate Semehot, 8.1.
58. Genesis Rabbah 100 (64a)
59. Malina and Rohrbaugh, *John*, 201.
60. Keener, *John*, 850.
61. Burge, *John*, NIV Application, 317.
62. Burge, *John*, Bible Knowledge, 104.
63. Koester, *The Word of Life*, 123.
64. Burge, *John*, Bible Knowledge, 476–477.
65. Catherine Clark Kroeger and Mary J. Evans, eds., *The IVP Women's Bible Commentary* (Downers Grove, Ill.: InterVarsity, 2002), 539.
66. *Joseph and Aseneth*, 20.3.
67. Murray J. Harris, *John*, Exegetical Guide to the Greek New Testament (Nashville: B&H, 2015), 243.
68. Morris, *Gospel According to John*, 544.
69. Grant R. Osborne, *The Gospel of John*, Cornerstone Biblical Commentary, vol. 13 (Carol Stream, Ill.: Tyndale, 20017), 197.
70. John R. W. Stott, *Issues Facing Christians Today*, 4th ed. (Grand Rapids: Zondervan, 2006), 494.
71. Carter and Wredberg, *Exalting*, 265.
72. Koester, *The Word of Life*, 117.
73. Carson, *John*, 518.
74. Burge, *John*, NIV Application, 416.
75. Kruse, *John*, 323.
76. Morris, *Gospel According to John*, 595.
77. Burge, *John*, NIV Application, 426.
78. Lincoln, *John*, 405.

PHOTOS AND ILLUSTRATIONS

Todd Bolen/BiblePlaces.com: pp. 10, 11, 25, 27, 30, 56 (left), 71, 72, 74, 85, 101, 117, 138, 149, 150, 153, 161, 162, 177

Photo courtesy of Sean McDowell: p. 17

Matt Williams: pp. 32, 86, 88 (all)

Library of Congress, Prints & Photographs Division, LC-DIG-matpc: pp. 41, 43, 59, 118, 131, 146

Christ Healing the Paralytic at the Pool of Bethesda by Bartolome Murillo (1667–1670): p. 76

Illustration courtesy of Cristina Malais: p. 87

The Temptation of Christ by Gustave Dore (1865): p. 106

Craig Dunning/BiblePlaces.com: p. 134

Jesus Washing Peter's Feet by Ford Madox Brown (1852–1856): p. 166

The Metropolitan Museum of Art, Rogers Fund, 1950: p. 167

Shutterstock.com: MIA Studio (front cover); Kutlayev Dmitry; Rostislav_ Sedlacek; Bobby Bradley; LimitedFont; Paul Steven; Carlos E. Santa Maria (back cover L to R); tomertu, p. 12; Gino Santo Maria, 13; SyRud, 14; Artit Fongfung, 16; klublu, 17; irina2511, 26; Billion Photos, 29; DisobeyArt, 34; Bernhard Richter, 42; frankie's, 45; Stephen Denness, 46; Pemaphoto, 48; pathdoc, 49; Discha-AS, 56 (right); Zyonimir Atletic, (relief on the baptismal font in the church of Saint Matthew in Stitar, Croatia on August 27, 2015), 58; Roman Mikhailiuk, 60; Dream Perfection, 61; Photographee.eu, 62, 79; szefei, 64; Africa Studio, 65 (top), 120, 151; Toa55, 65 (bottom); Suzanne Tucker, 80; Mikhail Semenov, 89; Brian A Jackson, 90; Marcin Wos, 92; Oliver Le Moal, 93; Snova, 94; focal point, 104; ruskpp, 106; WDG Photo, 107; Rawpixel.com, 111; MP_P, 112; Dirk Ercken, 124; All kind of people, 125; Andrew Cline, 132; Rick Schroeppel, 135; Renata Sedmakova (fresco, Vienna, 1911), 137; SvetaZi, 139; Benoit Daoust, 148; stockcreations, 154; Nemeziya, 156; Lukas Gojda, 163; Carlos E. Santa Maria, 164; welcomia, 169; Anastasiia Marynych, 178; P-Kheawtasang, 180; aradaphotography, 184.

Maps by Michael Schmeling www.aridocean.com